D0953023

SENNETS
& TUCKETS

A Bernstein Celebration

SENNETS
& TUCKETS

A Bernstein Celebration

edited by

STEVEN LEDBETTER

THE BOSTON SYMPHONY ORCHESTRA
in association with
DAVID R. GODINE, PUBLISHER / BOSTON

First published in 1988 by
The Boston Symphony Orchestra, Inc.
Symphony Hall
301 Massachusetts Avenue
Boston, Massachusetts 02115

in association with

David R. Godine, Publisher, Inc.
Horticultural Hall
300 Massachusetts Avenue
Boston, Massachusetts 02115

The articles in this collection were printed by the permission of
the authors. Permission was granted to reprint the following
previously published articles: John Rockwell's "Bernstein
Triumphant" from the *New York Times*; Robert S. Clark's
"Congruent Odysseys" and Humphrey Burton's "Leonard
Bernstein: Video man" from the Museum of Broadcasting;
Bernstein's "The Principle of Hope" from his own book *Findings*,
from Amberson Enterprises, Inc., and Simon and Schuster, Inc.

The Leonard Bernstein Calendar and The Music of Leonard
Bernstein are printed here with permission by Jack Gottlieb and
Amberson Enterprises, Inc.

Library of Congress Catalog Card Number: 88-45504
ISBN: 0-87923-775-9

First Edition
Printed in the United States of America

My own introduction to Lenny came through the kindness of Olga Koussevitzky, the widow of the Maestro. She took me by the hand at Seranak, and we walked together on that beautiful lawn with its magical view. She wanted to meet me since I had just won the Koussevitzky prize at the Tanglewood Music Center. She then told me I must meet Leonard Bernstein and study with him. The meeting took place months later in Berlin, during the New York Philharmonic's tour, and I became one of Lenny's assistants at the Philharmonic in 1961. Ever since then he has been for me, as for so many of us, an inspiring leader and colleague.

It is especially appropriate that this milestone, Lenny's seventieth birthday, be celebrated at Tanglewood, the place of our shared heritage, which he loves so deeply. I am happy that this volume will stand as a tribute to the unique place he occupies in our hearts.
With all our love and affection,
Happy Birthday Lenny!

Seiji Ozawa

Foreword

LEONARD BERNSTEIN had begun his passionate lifelong attachment to music well before coming to Tanglewood in the summer of 1940 as a member of the first class of the Berkshire (now Tanglewood) Music Center. And he had already shown more than enough signs of great talent to permit an expectation of future success. But it was at Tanglewood—years before the thrilling day when he took over for an indisposed Bruno Walter to conduct a nationally broadcast New York Philharmonic concert, years before the rousing success of his ballet *Fancy Free* or his first Broadway show *On the Town*— that Bernstein's career truly began.

At Tanglewood, Bernstein became Serge Koussevitzky's right hand and began to learn, in the school of experience, the art of conducting; at Tanglewood began one of our century's most distinguished careers on the podium. At Tanglewood Bernstein composed and heard his works performed. At Tanglewood he first conducted an opera. And to Tanglewood he has returned year after year as teacher and mentor to generations of young musicians, some of whom are able to attend the Music Center through fellowships that he himself has underwritten.

No other musician in American history has touched so many people at so many levels of musical experience. His audience ranges from the child whose first televised concert includes Bernstein's clear-sighted, accessible explanations, to the professional performer at the highest level of international acclaim. This book is a celebration of Leonard Bernstein's contributions—as composer, conductor, teacher and mentor, recording artist, media personality and spokesman, and visionary—to our musical life.

The contributors have addressed, in some ways, the various aspects of Bernstein's work, though no book of this modest scope could begin to encompass the whole of it. The man has been tireless in his musical activities for a half-century and has attained a measure of success in *all* his specialties that few people reach in a single one.

Throughout this half-century, which has included some of the darkest incidents of human history, Leonard Bernstein has retained an affirmative view that looks to the future with hope, that seeks in music and the other arts an expression of humanity's highest aspirations; these he has constantly held up to the young as a beacon and an inspiration. The ideals thus espoused are given verbal expression in his lecture "The Principle of Hope," delivered at the thirtieth anniversary of the Berkshire Music Center and reprinted in this volume.

The following pages range widely over the various elements of Bernstein's career, yet there is without question an emphasis on Tanglewood and Tanglewood connections. Given the central position of the Music Center in Bernstein's own career, and the role he has played in the fostering of others' careers through Tanglewood, we make no apology for the emphasis on that aspect of his life in the pages that follow.

Not surprisingly, Bernstein has long considered Tanglewood his artistic home, virtually hallowed ground for him as a musical artist. He decided to return there to celebrate his seventieth birthday, August 25, 1988, with a gala performance planned as a benefit for the endowment of the Tanglewood Music Center, and he noted on the letter sent to his friends inviting them to attend, "In my end is my beginning." The reference, from "East Coker," one of T. S. Eliot's *Four Quartets*, summarizes his feeling that this place is both destination and starting point.

Like the proceeds from the musical events on that occasion, the royalties from the sale of this book will go to the endowment of the Tanglewood Music Center, to assure the continuation of this master class of the musical arts.

*   *   *

As editor of this book, I must express my deepest gratitude to those authors who wrote articles especially for the volume as a contribution to the Tanglewood Music Center and in celebration of Bernstein.

Special thanks go also to those who granted permission to reprint previously published materials: to the *New York Times* for John Rockwell's article, "Bernstein Triumphant," from the *New York Times Magazine* of August 31, 1986, and to the author for revising the article for this volume; to the Museum of Broadcasting, its director Robert Batscha, and authors Robert S. Clark and Humphrey Burton, for permission to reprint their contributions to *Leonard Bernstein: The Television Work*, a catalogue published in conjunction with a special Bernstein exhibition at the museum in the fall of 1985; and to Amberson Enterprises, Inc., as well as Simon & Schuster, Inc., for permission to reprint "The Principle of Hope" from Leonard Bernstein's *Findings*. Thanks also to THEME Software Company for providing camera ready copy of the musical examples in my article.

Although *Sennets and Tuckets* is in no sense an "official" study of Leonard Bernstein, its completion would not have been possible without the generous cooperation of Amberson Enterprises, Inc., including Harry Kraut, Jack Gottlieb, and Charlie Harmon, who answered many questions and made available photographs, copies of manuscripts, and reference material.

Thanks are due, finally, to all those on the staff of the Boston Symphony Orchestra and the Tanglewood Music Center who served as source of ideas and as sounding-board while the book was gestating, and to designer Peter Carr, editor André Bernard, managing editor Lucinda Hitchcock, copy editor Lucy Ferriss, and the production staff at David R. Godine, Publisher, for the care, skill, professionalism, and dispatch with which they worked under the most hairraising of deadlines.

Steven Ledbetter
May 1988

Contents

SENNETS & TUCKETS

A Bernstein Celebration

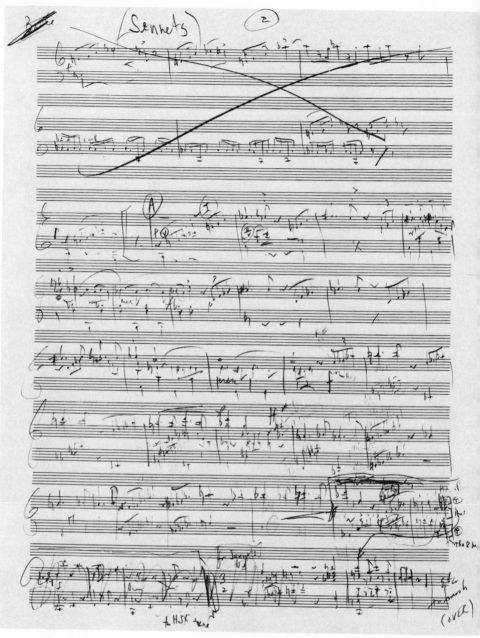

Sketch for "Sennets and Tuckets," the first movement of
Divertimento for Orchestra, *1980*

1

The Cultural Phenomenon

America has had her musical icons before, be they creator, performer, or spokesperson. Leonard Bernstein is by no means the first composer to write successfully for both the concert hall and the popular musical theater. In that regard he was anticipated by Victor Herbert, who was also highly regarded as a conductor.

Nor is he the first serious musician to have made a name for himself as explicator of music to the masses. In our time, Deems Taylor enjoyed an extended career as musical commentator to the general public in the press and on the radio, and the tradition goes back well into the last century, when the leading lights of the concert world—men like composer George Chadwick and conductor B.J. Lang—offered popular lectures on the repertory to be heard at the concerts of the Boston Symphony Orchestra.

He is, of course, in no way the first conductor to have a busy career in the recording studios, for there have been star conductors since the mid-1920s, when the development of the microphone made the recording of full orchestras a practical proposition.

But Bernstein has been uniquely able to multiply the effect of his many potent gifts—as pianist, conductor, composer for the concert hall and the theater, public speaker and lecturer, coach, teacher and mentor—through his own seemingly boundless energy and the lucky coincidental development of the electronic media that have spread his work more widely than was ever before possible.

At seventy, he epitomizes America's musical life in the eyes of the world.

Bernstein Triumphant

by JOHN ROCKWELL

IN a wash of weepy emotion, Leonard Bernstein stepped down as music director of the New York Philharmonic in 1969 and assumed the title "laureate conductor." Laureates sometimes carry with them an air of doddering grandeur. But at the age of fifty, Bernstein was still full of fire, fueled mostly by his ambitions to fulfill his interrupted promise as a composer.

Instead, the 1970s turned into Leonard Bernstein's personal Diaspora. Early on in his retirement, he was publicly mocked for his supposedly "radical chic" socializing at his home with the Black Panthers. His compositions came haltingly and were generally derided. He seemed caught up in a manic round of guest-conducting, mostly in Europe. His personal life was marked by the death in 1978 of his wife, the Chilean actress Felicia Montealegre. They had separated just before she was diagnosed as having cancer, and though they reconciled, Bernstein wondered aloud whether their troubles had somehow precipitated her illness. After her death, there was a period of depression, then giddy flamboyance. From having been the central figure in American musical life, Bernstein seemed dangerously close to grotesque self-parody.

John Rockwell has been a music critic on the staff of the *New York Times* since 1972. His interest in cultural history, the field in which he earned his Ph.D. at the University of California at Berkeley, is demonstrated in his 1983 book *All American Music* (Knopf), a series of essays on the current musical scene ranging from the avant-garde to jazz and pop.

But any dismissal of Bernstein was premature. He seems now, at long last, the magisterial presence his grandiose Philharmonic title implied nineteen years ago. His conducting has attained a new level of recognition—many critics, this one included, would be hard pressed to think of another conductor they would rather hear in the mainstream orchestral repertory. Bernstein's concerts earn the sort of adulation only true musical icons receive, and his seventieth birthday celebrations should only cap that acclaim.

While his composing must still be judged uneven, his old pieces sound better than ever: the New York City Opera's production and recording of *Candide* met with high praise, and his album of *West Side Story* topped the classical record sales charts. His work as a whole can now, in the climate of the "New Romantic" movement, be appreciated from a more sympathetic perspective, and he is showing signs of achieving, at seventy, a new balance in his personal life as well—despite sometimes embarrassing, sometimes wonderful lapses into emotionality.

It is that quite remarkable personality, for better and for worse, that defines every aspect of his near-manic existence. There are those who still find him inherently annoying—when he shoots off what he likes to call his "big Jewish mouth," when he prances and gyrates on the podium, when he seems to squander his compositional gifts in flashy trivia or overwrought excess. By his own admission an "embracing type," Bernstein hugs and kisses on all occasions, and his response to any hint of resistance from a huggee is to hug all the harder. Yet he seems so convinced of the value of such contact ("Some people have gender problems and sexual problems; some of them never even touched their parents; we talk about it later and they change and I'm rewarded"), that the easiest recourse is to hug him right back.

The one thing he cannot be accused of is insincerity. If anything, Bernstein has a surfeit of sincerity—he feels so extravagantly, and so wants *us* to feel with equal intensity, that he goes overboard. But in going up to and past the limit, he takes risks and achieves goals most others can't even imagine.

Like many artists, Bernstein is prone to deep depressions and wild upswings. Two summers ago, for instance, his mood was euphoric. At the Fairfield, Connecticut, country home he has had for twenty-seven years, he was typically juggling several balls at once. He was finishing *Jubilee Games*, and his oldest friend, Sid Ramin, whom he

Bernstein composing in his New York apartment, March 1945

Rehearsing the Berkshire Music Center Orchestra, August 1955

has known since he was twelve and who has orchestrated several of his Broadway scores, was helping him with the second movement. Bernstein was boning up on Sibelius's Second Symphony prior to conducting it with the young Tanglewood Music Center Orchestra and recording it with the Vienna Philharmonic. And two of his three children were in for the weekend—the then twenty-four-year-old Nina and thirty-one-year-old Alexander, both actors. The eldest, Jamie, a thirty-three-year-old rock composer and performer, was due to arrive the next day, and Bernstein, having just learned that she was going to make him a grandfather for the first time, was thrilled.

Years ago, Bernstein spoke admiringly of the image of old Picasso in the south of France, near-naked in his bikini and unfettered by bourgeois conventions. But despite his campy excesses, Bernstein remains very much the family man; the bonds between father and children are deep. When Nina arrived in her father's crowded dressing room after a Tanglewood concert a few days later, Bernstein looked up at her affectionately and said, "Hello, critter." "Hello, creature," she answered. It was a moment—a quiet place, if you will—of such simplicity that it validated his most extreme emotionality.

Although it was Bernstein's wife who was known as the hostess, his social life has remained active since her death. He gives parties, both formal and informal, at his homes in the Dakota, the well-known apartment building on Manhattan's Upper West Side, and in Connecticut. His social circles include many young people—student musicians, his children, and their friends. But there are also contemporaries from the worlds of classical composition and performance, the theater, literature, and politics.

For a true insight into Bernstein's public side, Tanglewood provides an ideal setting. It was at Tanglewood, in 1940, that Bernstein, fresh from Harvard, found one of his key mentors, the Boston Symphony conductor Serge Koussevitzky. In recent years, he has gone there every summer for ten days to conduct the annual Serge and Olga Koussevitzky Memorial Concert with the Boston Symphony, to lead the Tanglewood Music Center Orchestra, and to teach.

At Tanglewood, Bernstein runs himself happily ragged. "It doesn't stop," he sighed one day, changing his soaked sweat shirt for another fresh one. But he would be desolate if it ever *did* stop. Gliding through the Tanglewood grounds in his beige Mercedes convertible with his assistant, Craig Urquhart, he waves royally to crowds of earnest music students snapping their Instamatics, asking for autographs and hoping for a word or two.

He once described his conversation, television programs, and even conducting as teaching. "I'm a closet rabbi," he has said. Seated on his rehearsal stool, peering out from the podium over his half-glasses, he indeed looks rabbinical—like his father, Samuel, a Boston beauty-supply merchant and Talmudic scholar from Russia.

The most interesting of Bernstein's orchestral rehearsals two summers ago came with the Tanglewood Music Center Orchestra, a group young enough to profit from his broader cultural asides, yet sophisticated enough to respond to technical fine-tuning. Bernstein walked on to fervent applause from the players. He was wearing a baby-blue sweater, jeans, cowboy boots, and a red handkerchief tucked into a rear pocket, a big grin creasing his tanned and still classically handsome face. His favorite verbal punctuation consisted of hortatory adjectives like "glorious," "perfect," "terrific," "beautiful," and "sensational," often delivered while he scrutinized the score for some item he intended to make even more sensational. "Great!" he cried to the basses. "Use the whole bow and you'll be even greater—*twice* as great!"

Bernstein's podium manner in private rehearsals is just as "choreographed" as in public performance; his contortions may be distracting, but they are neither premeditated nor false. In the performance of the Sibelius, just before a violent brass entrance, he jumped straight into the air, his legs tucked up under his body as though he were taking a cannonball dive (he said later he had no memory of it). At the students' party afterward—he stayed until 5 a.m., talking and dancing—one could gaze out onto the crowded dance floor and see bodies occasionally springing up above the throng. The students had incorporated "Lenny's Leap" into their dance routines.

Bernstein's customary blend of analytical rigor, emotional fervor, and psychological cunning showed up in every rehearsal. His comment, "It's always thematic; you never have the sense you're playing unimportant stuff—that's Sibelius's glory as a symphonist," simultaneously reveals something very true about the composer's genius and serves to inspire performers who might otherwise lapse into boredom.

"Rule Number One in orchestral playing is: it's all chamber music," Bernstein said, whipping his glasses off and on again to conduct and examine the score. It was a remark he must have made thousands

*"Lenny's Flexible Cats"—Bernstein displays shirt given to him
by the 1986 Tanglewood Music Center Orchestra*

of times, but it remains vital. "Think dark, even when you're playing high," he cried, trying to elicit a Nordic feeling. "You can make a diminuendo on an upbeat—*you* don't think you can do it, but *I* tell you you can do it. . . . Thank you for that fortepiano; *Sibelius* thanks you. . . . Doesn't he say *tenuto* or something? Well, *I* say it; he *told* me to say it; we talk." To the first oboe: "This tiny entrance is like fifty trumpets." Then: "A great orchestra is a flexible orchestra: 'Lenny and his flexible cats.' . . . Pelvic pulse; excuse the expression, but that's what it is. *Passion*. . . . Now it's really throbbing; the whole orchestra is alive with this throb. . . . You gotta cry and suffer and that upbeat is part of it. . . . I love you; what can I say? You're just terrific."

When Bernstein first came to the Philharmonic, observers regularly complained about his exaggerations and superficiality, his application of a Broadway sensibility to the classics. Some of that may have been mere snobbery. But Bernstein himself concedes that he used to "over-conduct," punching home seductive details at the expense of an overall conception, and that his repertory and interpretation were too imitative of his teachers. These days, the details remain just as transparent, with more sensuous niceties than ever, but now they are nearly always subordinated to a vision of the entire piece.

Bernstein attributes some of his recent success to the orchestras with which he regularly works—the New York Philharmonic, the Boston Symphony, the Israel Philharmonic, the Bavarian Radio Symphony in Munich, and the Vienna Philharmonic. The linkage of this last ensemble to its "local" repertory of Haydn, Mozart, Beethoven, Schubert, Brahms, and Bruckner has lent a new weight to his realizations of the core repertory: the Viennese players steady him, he enlivens them. "You either get better or you die," he says. "To stick in a groove is an illness. I *hope* I've gotten better. What's the point of all the agony and the bliss and the study and the chameleon-like changing into Beethoven or Brahms or Schubert, otherwise?"

Orchestras today are routinely overworked and turn in routine performances as a result. Bernstein's status entitles him to extra rehearsals: for most Boston Symphony Tanglewood concerts, conductors get two rehearsals totaling five hours. For the Koussevitzky concert, with only two pieces on the program, Bernstein got three rehearsals and more than an hour of overtime, for a total of nearly nine hours. One could hear the difference—even wizened veterans respond to his care and passionate conviction.

In years past, his reputation as a conductor suffered because he didn't fit neatly into any of the then-prevalent categories. He was neither a brooding German mystic like Wilhelm Furtwängler nor a brisk, intense literalist like Arturo Toscanini. Bernstein's initial inspirations were the subjective emotionalism of Koussevitzky, with his commitment to unfashionable modern music; the strict discipline of Fritz Reiner; and the erratic but, at its best, incandescent blend of emotion and intellect of Dmitri Mitropoulos, who first implanted in the "genius boy" (as Mitropoulos called him) the notion that he could conduct. Bernstein honors his past, almost to the point of fetishism. When he conducts, he wears Koussevitzky's cuff links (he got married wearing Koussevitzky's white suit) and a Picasso dove of peace that Mitropoulos wore around his neck (this last is linked to a gold-plated shekel dating from 66 A.D. from Bernstein's wife).

Another secret to his success—and here his decision to give up the Philharmonic comes into its own—is that he is no longer a full-time conductor. He accepts those projects that attract him through his own organization, Amberson Productions, the name being a play on the English word for Bernstein, amber. Amberson is run by Harry Kraut, who is his "manager," if any person can be said to manage such a self-managed person; Kraut took over from Schuyler Chapin when Chapin went on to run the Metropolitan Opera. One of the things Bernstein and Kraut pay most attention to is blocking out time for composing. Bernstein took 1964–65 as a sabbatical from the Philharmonic, and 1980 was entirely devoted to composition. Usually, the stolen time comes in two- to four-month chunks, meaning he isn't mired in the day-to-day routines of conductors who only conduct.

Most of history's great conductors have been composers, bringing a special insight of their own time to their interpretations of music from other times. This tradition has deteriorated in recent decades as avant-garde composers have either given up the orchestra altogether or have composed in idioms too abstruse for audiences to understand and too complex for orchestras to play. Bernstein comes from a tonal American symphonic tradition, one to which most audiences can still relate, and he conducts the classics with a present-day rhythmic alacrity and a sense of color and drama that most other conductors, aping one past conducting style or another, grievously lack.

But if his composing freshens his conducting, Bernstein is not so sure the reverse is true. During his eleven-year Philharmonic tenure, he was able to complete only two major works—the *Kaddish* Symphony of 1963 and the *Chichester Psalms* of 1965. In the 1970s, he began with *Mass*, his closest approach to rock and a work dismissed by many critics. He then took time to prepare the Charles Eliot Norton Lectures at Harvard for 1973—a sometimes too breezily argued yet impassioned defense of tonality and eclecticism. After that came *The Dybbuk* in 1974, an ambitious but problematic ballet with Jerome Robbins, and *1600 Pennsylvania Avenue*, a disastrous Bicentennial musical about the White House. In 1977, there was the rather more successful *Songfest*, a compendium of poems and musical styles designed to honor the outsiders of American culture. Throughout this period, there was also a host of abandoned projects and occasional pieces and, finally, the opera *A Quiet Place* in 1983. This attempt at a sequel to his brief domestic drama of 1952, *Trouble in Tahiti*, was widely attacked as maudlin and melodramatic. Yet in its revised 1984 version, with the older opera embedded in the new material as flashbacks, one can imagine a successful production in a properly intimate theater.

Bernstein himself clearly feels a deep sense of disappointment as a composer. When Stephen Wadsworth, his *Quiet Place* librettist, didn't have time to undertake the libretto for their next operatic project, a five-language vision of the Holocaust, Bernstein was devastated. One problem is an increasingly rigorous sense of self-criticism—or, one suspects, self-doubt. "I've always thrown stuff away," he says, "but I throw a lot more now. I've thrown it away for the same reason—it's dishonest, it's not me, it's there for some specious reason that I may not even know myself."

Another difficulty is freeing himself of his involvement with the music of others. The first part of any composing period, he complains, is spent purging the composers he has been conducting, and the last part in re-entering other composers' psyches as he studies their scores for forthcoming performances. "When I really study a score, I recompose it along with the composer," he says. "It takes so much time and so much psychic energy, it's almost schizoid. It takes two weeks to get those other guys out of my head—Ives and Haydn and Copland and Brahms. *Then* maybe I can go about finding my own notes. At first, even if you find what you *think* are your notes, you don't trust them. It's painful."

There are those who feel he has never escaped those other voices—that his music is at its core derivative. Back in 1949, his old mentor and friend Aaron Copland, of all people, wrote that "at its worst, Bernstein's music is conductors' music—eclectic in style and facile in inspiration." Add to that a tendency toward soul-searching affirmations of verities that veer dangerously close to clichés—pious conventionalities masquerading as archetypes.

Set against such doubts—his own and others'—are his music's palpable virtues. He has a moving melodic gift, something especially rare in our time. Tunes such as "Somewhere" from *West Side Story* or the big theme from *Trouble in Tahiti* rank him very high indeed. His vernacularly inspired rhythmic dash and syncopated swagger, and the theatrical directness and accessibility of even his most ostensibly "serious" scores, make him a composer of undeniable gifts and popular appeal. But during the 1950s and '60s, Bernstein's deeply conservative adherence to tonal tradition—the precise opposite of his reputation for trendiness—put him at odds with vanguard composers including Stravinsky and Copland. Now, in a climate of "New Romanticism," Bernstein begins to look like a prophet. That's why he's so proud of his Harvard lectures, with their affirmation of tonality as based on universal law. "I don't feel vindicated as a composer," he says. "But I do as a lecturer, as a teacher."

Yet there is more to Bernstein's music than a mere dogged adherence to tonality. He brings an irresistible flavor of popular music and jazz to his symphonic scores, and that still gets him into trouble with conservative critics who might otherwise applaud his harmonic traditionalism. He would surely have enjoyed a more straightforward success if he had stuck to Broadway after the triumph of *West Side Story* in 1957. All the plaudits that have accrued to Stephen Sondheim, his one-time librettist and avowed disciple, might have fallen on him. Instead, Bernstein took on the Philharmonic and continued his perhaps futile, yet still noble attempt to inject the spirit of the vernacular into the classical tradition. In this sense, his most extreme and interesting work has been *Mass*, and its rejection caused him much bitterness. Compared with eighteenth- and nineteenth-century Masses, Bernstein's work sounds bizarre. In its proper context, as a fusion of classical music, Broadway, and the nascent rock musical, it is remarkable.

All his life, Bernstein has championed the idea that it is imperative for an American composer, caught up in our welter of culture influences, to be an eclectic. "Why is that word pejorative?" he wonders. It is just this blending of popular and "serious" styles, and his willingness to leap wildly from style to style within a given score, that incurs the greatest musical antagonism. But it should be remembered that Mahler—"the most original mind of his time," says Bernstein—was rejected for decades because of this seemingly incongruous mishmash of styles and excess of emotion. Bernstein may not be Mahler. But one suspects his time will come, too, and for much the same reasons—people will accept the emotionality and cherish the diversity.

One reason tonal, accessible music is back in fashion is the conservative cultural and political climate of the Western world. Ironically, the vilification of Bernstein for "radical chic" was a harbinger of this reaction, with protests that he is sure were organized by the F.B.I. to discredit his liberalism and to drive a wedge between the Jewish and black communities.

If Bernstein has been wandering in a lonely Diaspora since the 1970s, part of the reason has been his sense of alienation from the conservative mainstream. Bernstein remains an unregenerated liberal, a fighter for minority rights and for peace. A friend of Democratic presidents, he was last in the White House—"my favorite house in the whole world"—in the waning days of the Carter presidency, when he managed to "sneak" twenty-one members of his entourage and family into Lincoln's bedroom to recite Jewish prayers. He has not been there since, and says he won't go while Reagan remains in office.

Such commitment to principle and to his Jewish faith might seem to pose him an enormous problem. He loves the Vienna Philharmonic, but many American Jewish leaders have advocated some sort of boycott of Austria now that Kurt Waldheim, accused by some of covering up his Nazi past, is that country's president. What was Leonard Bernstein, a powerful symbol of American Jewish achievement, to do? He decided to march back to Vienna to show the colors.

"I think not to go back is retreat," he argued. "I *am* going to go back, because the musicians are my brothers, my Brüderlein—I love them. Not to go would be abandoning them. It would be like *rejecting* them, because of the ghastly Waldheim thing. It doesn't *matter* if he was a criminal—that's water under the bridge. But that he spent as much effort *forging* an autobiography, and then on top of all that *totally* lying—he has the nerve, the *chutzpah*, to run for the presidency of his country, knowing full well his main support comes from ex-Nazis, or not even *ex*-Nazis."

Eventually Bernstein would like to write his autobiography, utterly candid and for publication only after his death. But having given up trying to type it into a computer, he is looking for a collaborator. Additional motivation for telling his side of his story comes from the tell-all biography by Joan Peyser, which he "dreaded," with its revelations of his homosexuality and its blunt speculations about his psychological makeup and its relation to his work.

But in the end, for this most instinctive and gregarious of collaborators, everything returns to the solitary, lonely act of composition. Bernstein works in the studio his wife fashioned for him from an old barn in back of the Fairfield house. Most of his memorabilia are in a Manhattan studio, where for years they were presided over by Helen Coates, his former piano teacher (when he was fourteen years old) and long-time secretary, now eighty-nine and in poor health. Along with his mother, now ninety, Helen Coates represents the last link with the previous generation.

But there is plenty of memorabilia in Connecticut, too—pictures of a wife he still describes with sudden, passionate intensity as "the greatest person I ever met in my life," of his mentors and idols. There are Grammy awards, a grand piano, a sitdown desk and a standup shelf where he does his actual composing (unless you count the couch—he swears the real work comes at night, when he's prone).

Although he seems in ruddy good health, Bernstein has reason to worry. Always asthmatic and prone to emphysema, he remains a mercilessly heavy smoker. "The great thing about conducting," he says, "is that you don't smoke and you breathe in great gobs of oxygen. When I sit around for months and compose, I get bronchitis." At times he is afflicted with a racking cough that makes his friends wince, and he constantly has to clear his throat. At Alan Jay Lerner's memorial service, people outside held up a sign saying, "We love you—stop smoking."

Beyond all that, more and more friends are dying from those natural causes that begin to touch everyone at his age. And an entire younger set of friends is falling to acquired immune deficiency syndrome. Bernstein says he spent an agonizing time on a European tour recently trying to make telephone contact with a young conducting student who was dying of AIDS and whose family was profoundly

Conducting the Tanglewood Music Center Orchestra from the keyboard

embarrassed by any of his friends' attempting to contact him. "It was terrible—he was absolutely pure, this boy. When I was finally put through to him, he said everything was wonderful: he felt better, he was gaining weight. Right after that, he died."

On August 25, 1988, Bernstein will be seventy years old, the biblical lifespan beyond which all time is borrowed from God. "My father was seventy in 1962, and there was a huge party for him in Boston," he recalls. "The whole family was there, the Mayor and other politicians—it was the high point of his life. But already he was worried. After that he declined steadily, and finally died in 1969." The implication is clear: Bernstein feels driven to accomplish whatever he hopes to accomplish, soon.

But all that might seem too downbeat for a man who still has the seductive charm and youthful vitality of an ageless boy wonder. After a couple of weeks with him, watching him in action and thinking about his life, one finds oneself wishing that he can knit it all together, that he can achieve his lifelong goal of combining the classical and popular, traditional and daring, creative and re-creative, intellectual and emotional, social and solitary. He has given us a lot; here's hoping there will be more for years to come.

Jeremiah *Symphony*—*pencil short score of the opening movement with dedication to Renée Longy and added note with date of "Premiere via Fritz [Reiner]"*

Tanglewood Beginnings

*When the Berkshire Music Center started in 1940, it was the fulfill-
ment of Serge Koussevitzky's lifelong dream of a school for advanced
training for musicians on the verge of professional careers. It must
have been difficult to be confident of the future in that summer, with
the clouds of a European war already darkening the horizon in
America. Referring to the situation in his opening address to the
fellows invited to attend the Music Center, Koussevitzky reaffirmed
the central role of the arts, and especially of music, in preserving
civilization and humanity at such a time.*

*What no one could have foreseen was the powerful role that so
many of the young musicians in that first Tanglewood class were
destined to play in American musical life, as composers, conductors,
instrumentalists, singers, teachers, and administrators. Hope was
high, and it was a hope that, amply fulfilled, provided the model for
years to come.*

*For a great many of those young musicians, the summer of 1940
opened a door to the future.*

First Summer

by ANDREW L. PINCUS

H AROLD SHAPERO remembers the dormitory room as a musical madhouse. Leonard Bernstein was working on his scores for his next session with Koussevitzky, and Shapero was supposed to be composing. Meanwhile, cellist Arthur Winograd, bassist Henry Portnoi and clarinetist Nathaniel Brusilow were trying to practice.

Like any good conducting student, Bernstein wasn't content to pore over the mysteries contained in the notes. He had to hear the music somehow, and there was no piano in the room—only what Shapero recalls as "one ratty little upright downstairs" there at the Cranwell School for boys, where Tanglewood's male students roomed.

"So in the room," Shapero says, "[Bernstein] was screaming and yelling at his scores and singing all the parts. And Portnoi was getting his bass going and Brusilow was whacking away at the clarinet and Winograd had this hilarious way of playing the cello—he would borrow people's fiddles and play them like cellos, standing them up like a little cello. And I didn't make much noise but I couldn't conceivably compose." Shapero complained to Paul Hindemith, who "went running" to Aaron Copland, who said, "That Shapero's impossible. Throw him out."

"That's the room I remember," Shapero says.

It was the first summer of the Berkshire (now Tanglewood) Music Center, 1940—Bernstein's first summer at Tanglewood. One of his four fellow conducting students, and Koussevitzky's other favorite, was Lukas Foss, a refugee from Europe, four years younger than the

Music critic of the *Berkshire Eagle*, Andrew L. Pincus has covered many Tanglewood seasons. He is completing a book on Tanglewood to be published in 1989 by Northeastern University Press.

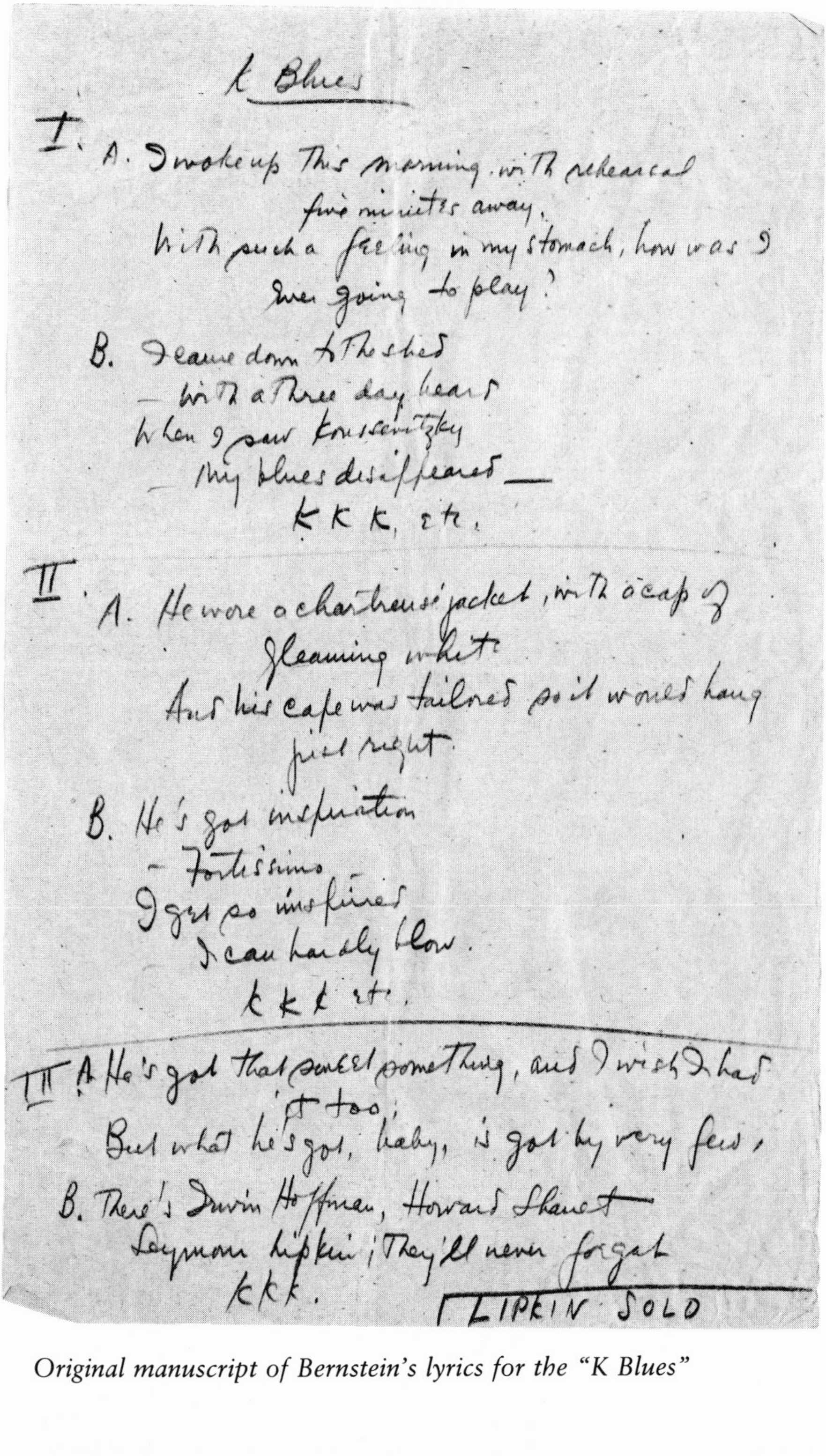
K Blues

I. A. I woke up this morning with rehearsal
five minutes away.
With such a feeling in my stomach, how was I
ever going to play?

B. I came down to the shed
— with a three day beard
When I saw Koussevitzky
— my blues disappeared —
KKK, etc.

II. A. He wore a chartreuse jacket, with a cap of
gleaming white
And his cape was tailored so it would hang
just right.

B. He's got inspiration
— Fortissimo
I get so inspired
I can hardly blow.
KKK etc.

III A. He's got that sweet something, and I wish I had
it too;
But what he's got, baby, is got by very few,

B. There's Irwin Hoffman, Howard Shanet
Seymour Lipkin; they'll never forget
KKK.
LIPKIN SOLO

Original manuscript of Bernstein's lyrics for the "K Blues"

IV. A. He played the Fourth of Brahms, and he gave it
   all he's got:
  It started twenty below zero, but it wound up
   awful hot.

 B. So remember, baby, in the Fourth of Brahms
  No matter how piano, it must have "just stance" —
   k k k , etc .

        └ HOFFMAN SOLO

V. A. I've got those Koussevitzky blues, and, baby,
   That ain't good :
  'Cause he's the best dressed man in all of
   Tanglewood.

 B. We wear dungarees, we dress like apes,
  But come the Revolution we'll all wear capes —
   k k k —

        └ SHANET SOLO

VI. A. So Dr. Koussevitzky, long life and health
   to you :
  To Madame Koussevitzky, and Mrs. Hirschmann
   too.

 B. There's conductors in the East, Conductors in the West,
  But we got Koussevitzky, and we're stuck with
   The best
  k k k – etc . ———— Oh Serge Alexandrovich !

*Performance of the "K Blues" on the porch of the Main House
at Tanglewood, July 26, 1948 (left to right: Irwin Hoffman,
violin; Howard Shanet, cello; Seymour Lipkin, piano; Leonard
Bernstein, vocalist)*

worldly twenty-one-year-old from Harvard and the Curtis Institute. Foss remembers looking up to Bernstein as "an older brother" who explained jokes to him, taught him to love Gershwin, and helped him with his English pronunciation. Koussevitzky, Foss says, once described the pair of them—to his barber, no less—as the two "who are going places," one "Apollonian," the other "Dionysian." After deciding "I was much too shy to be Dionysian," Foss yielded the Bacchic honor to his idol.

On another note, Foss recalls the "Koussevitzky Blues," which Bernstein composed and then sang from the piano at a Seranak birthday party for the old man. The refrain, alluding to Koussevitzky's preferred mode of dress, went:

> *Some of us wear jeans and some dress like apes,*
> *But comes the revolution and we all wear capes.*
> *Koussey! Koussey! Koussey!*

Koussevitzky loved it and laughed as hard as the other revelers on that happy day, Foss says. The piece, in fact, hung on as a feature of Koussevitzky birthday celebrations in later years.

Carlos Moseley, a piano student in 1941 and later Bernstein's comrade in arms as managing director (and, later still, president) of the New York Philharmonic, remembers playing the first movement of Brahms's B-flat Piano Concerto with the Music Center Orchestra under Bernstein.

"It was great working with him," Moseley says. "He was marvelous in those days. There was a lot of excitement any time he conducted. Even though he was a student, he was the outstanding student, of course, and there was a great deal of talk about him." At a rehearsal for Constant Lambert's *Rio Grande* for piano, chorus, and orchestra, for instance, "Everybody was remarking how well he had been able to teach the student orchestra the rhythmic patterns and other things that were there. He was just so much better than everybody else."

Bernstein's sister, Shirley, who visited him regularly, also fell under the spell. She recalls "happiness and going to eat late at night, singing and music, and just very gay, wonderful times. We were always piling into cars and driving off to some hamburger joint." Or, as Lukas Foss puts it, Bernstein "was sort of elegant and well-behaved" in those days. "The shocking things came much, much later."

The Maestro, of course, has been at Tanglewood as a student,

Tanglewood consultation: Tod Perry, Aaron Copland, Leonard Bernstein, 1948

teacher, composer, pianist, conductor or some combination of those things nearly every summer since Koussevitzky realized his vision of a summer academy for musicians in America. The first three summers, however, were his student years. By 1943 the war had shut down Tanglewood except for some chamber and small-orchestra concerts, and when the music sounded again in full glory in 1946, Bernstein was back as Koussevitzky's assistant, conducting, among other things, the American premiere of Benjamin Britten's *Peter Grimes*.

Friends and classmates knew from the start that the young man from Lawrence, Massachusetts, was marked for greatness. Thomas D. Perry, Jr., who was in the student opera program in 1940 and went on to become the BSO's executive director, was impressed not only by the talent but also by the industry. Says Perry: "He was terribly busy and he was obviously a very gifted person. It's been written all over him that he's a genius since he was a kid. He was a hard-working man. He was obviously the leader of the [conducting] students."

Many of Bernstein's fellow students knew him in and around Boston before Tanglewood. To them, too, the talent—and what everyone later would recognize as the loyalty to friends—was unmistakable. One of those friends, now as then, is BSO violist Jerome Lipson, who was Bernstein's classmate at Boston Latin School.

"He was my accompanist in school," Lipson recalls. "I would play solos occasionally in the assembly hall and he would be at the piano. When we graduated in 1935, I played the solo and he was my accompanist, and we were friends. We would go to a house party on a Friday night or Saturday night and it would always end up the same way. He'd be at the piano, playing and talking, everybody listening to him because he had that much to say."

Lipson also spent time with Bernstein during summers at Sharon, a resort town south of Boston, where their families had nearby cottages on the lake. This was during the depths of the Depression, of course. One day Lipson and Bernstein had a talk about what they were going to do with their lives. Lipson recalls:

"I was walking home with him. He said, 'What are you going to be when you grow up? I'm going to be a piano player.' And I said, 'Where are you going to go from here?' And he said, 'Well, I'm going to go to the Curtis Institute.' And I said, 'What's that?' in my ignorance. He said, 'Well, that's the best school there is, and besides you can't pay to go there. You don't have to and you can't.' And I said, 'Good. I'll go there.' So on his advice I went, took the audition and ended up spending four years in Philadelphia."

From Boston Latin, however, Bernstein went not to Curtis but to Harvard, where he took a B.A. Although Bernstein carried out his Curtis plan after Harvard and studied conducting with Fritz Reiner there, the friends' paths did not cross again until Tanglewood. Lipson also spent the first three summers there as a student, playing in the orchestra under Bernstein.

The Music Center Orchestra's concert format then was the same as it is today, with the student conductors taking the first half of the program and the senior conductor—in those days Koussevitzky, of course—leading the major work after intermission. Lipson remembers a rehearsal at which Koussevitzky worked the orchestra from ten a.m. until twelve-forty p.m. With twenty minutes left in the allotted rehearsal time, Koussevitzky turned to Bernstein and said, "And now, *mein* dear, the rest of the time is yours." Bernstein, Lipson says, was "mad as hell" and protested until he got an hour of overtime. The overtime tradition, of course, remains alive and well today.

(Harold Shapero remembers another tumultuous rehearsal. Bernstein was conducting Rimsky-Korsakov's *Scheherazade*—one of the first pieces he did at Tanglewood. "When the cymbals come in with this tremendous crash," Shapero says, "Lenny acted out the crash on the podium with his hands. It was hilarious. We all gave him holy hell afterwards.")

Former BSO librarian Victor Alpert and his wife Dorothy, a violinist, also knew Bernstein from high-school days. Dorothy Alpert (then Dorothy Rosenberg), in fact, performed in the premiere of the budding composer's Opus 1, a trio. The year was about 1937, and the other performers, also friends of Bernstein's, were cellist Sarah Kruskall and pianist Mildred Spiegel. The premiere took place at a party in Boston for Bernstein's father. "It was a good piece—sort of light, easy," Dorothy Alpert recalls. "Some technically difficult places but on the whole very playable."

A few years later Dorothy was a student at the New England Conservatory and Bernstein, a freshly minted Harvard man, was living in an apartment across Huntington Avenue while trying to make his way in the world as a musician. She had an audition coming up with the conservatory director, at which she was to play the

Wieniawski D minor Concerto. At the last minute her accompanist canceled.

Frantic, she "went all over the place, looking for somebody" to fill in. Finally she found Bernstein across the street. He agreed to be the pianist. "He sight-read the Wieniawski," she recalls, still incredulous. "He had never played it before, and it was incredible the way he played the accompaniment. I got a good mark." The tale is one of many about the young pianist's sight-reading prowess.

Victor Alpert, a violinist who later switched to the viola, knew Bernstein from an all-Boston high school orchestra in which they performed together. Alpert was the concertmaster and Bernstein was the pianist. A performance of the Grieg Concerto, with Leonard Bernstein as the soloist, provided Alpert with his introduction to a piece he was destined to know well in his BSO years.

Like the Lipsons and Bernsteins, the Alpert family had a cottage by the lake in Sharon, a popular Jewish resort community. Alpert thus became one of the crowd of young people Bernstein recruited for the Gilbert and Sullivan—or as they called it, "Goldberg and Solomon"—performances he staged in the Town Hall while on summer vacations from Harvard. *The Mikado* and *H.M.S. Pinafore* were the two summers' shows, and the proceeds—about fifty dollars, Alpert thinks—went to charity. Bernstein assigned himself the lead roles of Nanki-Poo and Captain Corcoran. The premiere production, however, given in a hotel dining room, was a Carmen play that Bernstein had written with a Harvard friend. Alpert was the referee in a bullfight and Bernstein played Carmen. Lipson recalls that it was from his Aunt Sadie that Bernstein, taking great pride in doing so, borrowed Carmen's dress.

Both Alperts were at Tanglewood during 1940 and 1941, Dorothy as a student, Victor as Dorothy's beau in 1940 but as a student in his own right the next year. They, too, played under Bernstein in the student orchestra. Victor Alpert says Bernstein clearly stood out that first year among the student conductors, including Foss, Gaylord Browne, Richard Bales and Thor Johnson. To Dorothy Alpert, "It was a very exciting and thrilling experience to be sitting in the orchestra and playing for someone I knew so well."

Others who observed the young Bernstein during those yeasty years include Eugene Lehner, new in the BSO viola section in 1939 and now retired. He recalls that "Bernstein was inseparable from Koussey because Koussevitzky was absolutely taken by his talent, and he

Bernstein, Copland, Koussevitzy, August 1948

became a father to Bernstein." Viola Aliferis, whose former husband, James Aliferis, studied choral conducting under Hugh Ross the first year (and who was later to spend many years herself as a BSO staff member), says Bernstein "was just a great guy, very talented, just the way he is today." Helen Perry, Tod Perry's wife, who also was in the opera program in 1940, recalls a happy night just after Tanglewood that summer. Bernstein and William Schuman came to dinner at the Perry apartment on Beacon Street in Boston and played jazz piano "until the wee hours," to the dismay of neighbors. And everybody remembers the aftermath of the final rehearsal for Lambert's *Rio Grande*.

As Bernstein himself tells the story, Tallulah Bankhead, who was playing in summer stock nearby, turned up in the Shed during the rehearsal. Koussevitzky, glowing, took her backstage afterwards to introduce her to his protégé. Bankhead told Bernstein she had fallen in love with his back muscles and insisted on inviting him to dinner in her boardinghouse room in Stockbridge. With help from Bankhead's chauffeur, a "roaring drunk" Bernstein barely made it back to Tanglewood in time to navigate the *Rio Grande*'s difficult shoals at that night's concert.

Bernstein's other remembrances of the first summer are perhaps best expressed in a letter he sent back to his parents. In it he writes: " . . . I have never seen such a beautiful setup in my life. I've been conducting the orchestra every morning, & I'm playing my first concert tomorrow night. Kouss gave me the hardest & longest number of all—the Second Symphony of Randall Thompson. 30 minutes long—a modern American work—as my first performance. And Kouss is so pleased with my work. He likes me & works very hard with me in our private sessions. He is the most marvelous man—a beautiful spirit that never lags or fails—that inspires me terrifically. And he told me he is convinced that I have a wonderful gift, & he is already making me a great conductor. (I actually rode in his car with him today!). . . We've been working very hard—you're always going like mad here—no time to think of how tired you are or how little you slept last night—the inspiration of this Center is terrific enough to keep you going with no sleep at all. I'm so excited about tomorrow night—I wish you could all be here—it's so important to me—& Kouss is banking on it to convince him that he's right—if it goes well there's no telling what may happen. . . ."

What happened, of course, all the world knows. But others, like

Harold Shapero and Lukas Foss, remember later incidents that connect the mature Bernstein to the student they knew. Shapero, who overlapped with Bernstein at Harvard and now teaches at Brandeis University, recalls clowning around in the practice room and a later performance in New York at which—too busy or lazy to practice—they fobbed off their own compositions as Shostakovich's. But, after the jokes are done, Shapero remains grateful for an early hi-fi recording of his Symphony for Classical Orchestra that Bernstein made with the Columbia Symphony Orchestra.

Not only was that recording "the most important thing he ever did for me," says Shapero, but Bernstein, apparently down with the flu, went to the all-day recording session in New York with a fever of 102½. "And that son of a gun was in a state of physical collapse around noon, and he got into a cab and ran uptown and got a shot of penicillin or some other thing, and finished up. He was sick as a dog." It was a first-rate performance, Shapero says.

Foss and Bernstein also collaborated from time to time over the years, Bernstein conducting many of Foss's works—"He's done them so beautifully," Foss gratefully says—and Foss giving a major Bernstein festival three years ago with the Milwaukee Symphony, which he was then directing. Bernstein's tempos were much faster in his earlier days, even in his own works, Foss recalls.

When Foss performed Bernstein's *Chichester Psalms* in the Milwaukee festival, for instance, he followed the tempos in Bernstein's first recording of the work. Foss remembers Bernstein telling him, "It's much too fast," and denying he had ever recorded the music at any such speed. When the dust settled, it turned out Bernstein was talking about his second recording of the piece.

"It's amazing, you know," Foss says. "Somebody like that is good right from the start. And he also knew how to handle people, which I had to learn. It took me ten years [to learn], and he knew how to get the most from the musicians. I remember admiring that—how well he handled them at rehearsals, how he got results. He got results where I just knew my scores."

And that, as they say, is what makes a conductor.

*Lukas Foss and Leonard Bernstein in a two-piano recital at
Seranak (with Cornelia Foss and Felicia Bernstein turning pages)
for the benefit of the Stockbridge Bowl Association, 1953*

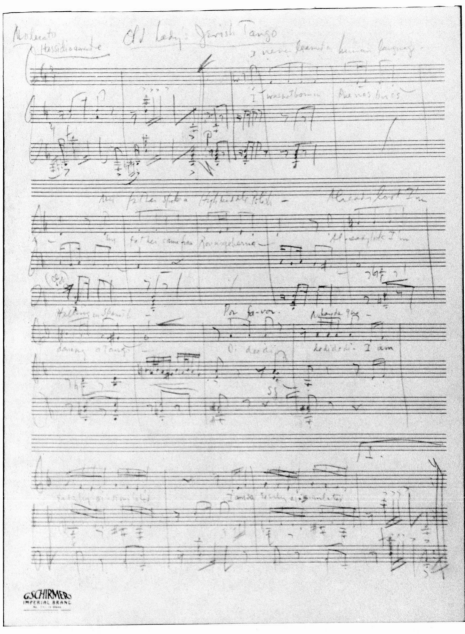

Candide, *fair copy piano-vocal score of the Old Lady's tango,*
"*I am easily assimilated,*" *1956*

3

Composer

By far the best-known compositions of Leonard Bernstein are for the popular theater. After starting with two zippy musical comedies about New York, On the Town *(1944) and* Wonderful Town *(1953)*, his full-fledged operetta Candide *(1956) was so filled with glorious music and terrific singing that its original cast recording remained an underground favorite even though the show itself died after seventy-three performances. It rose, phoenix-like, not once but three times: first to become a hit in a musically simplified but theatrically enlivened Broadway version (1973), then in a musically elaborate "opera-house version" (1982), and finally, in the composer's seventieth year, in a still larger "elaborate opera-house version" produced in Glasgow. And of course, the epochal West Side Story (1957) stretched the boundaries of the musical theater toward the seriousness of opera without ever denying the particular genius of the Broadway stage.*

But Bernstein has continuously worked in all areas of concert music: the theater (ballet, opera, and Mass, a work that is sui generis); the concert hall (three symphonies, concerted pieces for soloist and orchestra, choral compositions); and the recital hall (songs, solo and chamber works). He has ranged stylistically from the utmost simplicity to flirtations with the twelve-tone Muse (who has never succeeded in winning him over).*

These two broad categories of music are heard largely by different audiences, so it has been too easy to divide Bernstein's work as a composer into the isolated categories of "popular" and "serious" (or whatever invidious terms one might use) without noticing how much it is all of a piece, how responsive he has been to the variety and energy and color that abound in the American experience.*

Broadway's Mozartean Moment,

OR

An Amadeus in Amber

by LARRY STEMPEL

O N October 7, 1956, Leonard Bernstein appeared on television for the odd purpose of discussing music. To be sure, the oddness lay not so much in discussing music as in doing so—seriously—on television. Moreover, this was not the first time that Bernstein, using music to instruct rather than to entertain his audience, had laid siege to the "boob tube"; nor would it be the last. His first telecast, two years before, had been a riveting presentation of Beethoven's Fifth Symphony in words as well as tones. And from then on, he would find cause to return to the medium on occasion, seeking ever new ways to make accessible to a mass public such formidable topics as Bach, romanticism, grand opera, and modern music.

On this occasion, however, Bernstein chose to speak on a matter somewhat out of keeping with the rest. His subject was American musical comedy, a branch of show business which hardly seemed in need of an explanation at all. Indeed, musical comedy was a familiar American indulgence the vitality of which had already won a mass following through the hit songs that came from its hit shows. Less art than entertainment, moreover, the music of musical comedy also seemed unworthy of the same kind of respect and cultural consideration that Bernstein lavished televisually on the music of Beethoven and Bach.

In 1962, as a Tanglewood fellow, Larry Stempel studied composition with Witold Lutoslawski. He is now an associate professor of music at Fordham University, and is writing a book on the American musical theater for W. W. Norton & Company.

But that was precisely the point in taking to the airwaves. For it was Bernstein's intention to show how an entertainment made chiefly of pop tunes and low comedy had gradually acquired a high-minded seriousness of its own. So on this Sunday afternoon, after discussing the genre and giving his audience a tuneful smattering from the likes of Victor Herbert, the Gershwins, Irving Berlin, Cole Porter, and Rodgers and Hammerstein, he ended his telecast with these words:

> We are in a historical position now similar to that of the popular musical theater in Germany just before Mozart came along. In 1750, the big attraction was what they called the *Singspiel*, which was the *Annie Get Your Gun* of its day, star comic and all. This popular form took the leap to a work of art through the genius of Mozart. After all, *The Magic Flute* is a *Singspiel*; only it's by Mozart.
>
> We are in the same position; all we need is for our Mozart to come along. If and when he does, we surely won't get any *Magic Flute*; what we'll get will be a new form, and perhaps "opera" will be the wrong word for it. There must be a more exciting word for such an exciting event. And this event can happen any second. It's almost as though it is our moment in history, as if there is a historical necessity that gives us such a wealth of creative talent at this precise time.

How canny the speculation! How extravagant the claim! How cautious the qualification! Overlooking the differences of time and place, one could well consider a *Singspiel* an eighteenth-century sort of American musical comedy. Both were entertainments of the same kind, after all: native comic plays with musical numbers and spoken dialogue in between. But *The Magic Flute* was a *Singspiel* that so turned the genre around that Richard Wagner considered it the first great German opera. Since there was nothing quite like it in the history of American musical comedy, however—discounting *Porgy and Bess*, which was short on both spoken dialogue and comedy—Bernstein's parallel between the flowering of German opera and the state of the Broadway musical *circa* 1950 had an air of pretension about it. It would shortly prove to be a tad self-serving as well.

Though it may have seemed so to wishful thinkers at the time, the Broadway musical was not on the brink of some grand artistic transformation. On the contrary, it seems as though Broadway was nearing the end of what may well have been the period of its most brilliant musical creations for the stage. The great figures of Berlin (*Annie Get Your Gun*), Porter (*Kiss Me, Kate*), and Rodgers and Hammerstein (*Oklahoma!*; *Carousel*; *South Pacific*)—not to mention Frank Loesser (*Guys and Dolls*), Lerner and Loewe (*My Fair Lady*), and a host of others—were all still alive and working, yet their best achievements were already things of the past or fast becoming so by October 1956. Bernstein's final words on musical comedy, then, were more in the way of exhorting than reporting.

It is a coincidence, no doubt, that in 1775 the poet Christoph Martin Wieland had urged a similar role for the *Singspiel* itself in creating a new kind of German opera. He had done so, moreover, with no likely knowledge of what was in store, for years were to elapse before Mozart came along and wrote his greatest works in the genre: *The Abduction from the Seraglio* (1782) and *The Magic Flute* (1791). But late in 1956, Bernstein would go Wieland one better: it was not so much Broadway's musical "moment in history" as his own. Indeed, if it was historical necessity summoning the American musical theater upward as well as onward at the time, it was Bernstein himself who was on hand to answer the call—as he made ready not just his greatest scores for Broadway, but the works that would become of all his compositions perhaps the most admired, durable, and popular. Two months after his "American Musical Comedy" telecast, *Candide* opened on Broadway; ten months after that, *West Side Story*.

Now Bernstein was no stranger to the commercial stage. He had already provided Broadway with the scores to two hit musicals, *On the Town* (1944) and *Wonderful Town* (1953). And he was to return to Broadway one more time with the score for the venturesome *1600 Pennsylvania Avenue* (1976). The musical flopped, however, and, in an industry in which box-office receipts are the touchstone of success, the work has thus far been consigned to the status of historical curiosity. As for the successful two *Towns* (both singing the praises of one: New York), they were prime examples of honest-to-goodness musical comedy, put together under the supervision of Broadway's own master of the form, George Abbott. As much as they sparkled with a winning freshness of invention, these shows were hardly of the stuff for turning the genre around.

But *Candide* (1956) and *West Side Story* (1957) were something else. Filled with all manner of entertainment, they were nonetheless serious works that appeared somewhat out of place on the Broadway stage. Strange as it seems, the now classic *West Side Story* was slow at first to gain broad public acceptance, while *Candide* actually flopped in its original production, though later incarnations of the work have proved substantial hits. Speaking in Broadway terms, these shows resembled not musical *comedies* so much as musical *plays*.

The prestige of the "musical play" as a genre owes much to the influence of Oscar Hammerstein II. While he had already applied the term to his operetta scripts of the 1920s (*Rose Marie*; *Show Boat*), its modern use stems more from its connection with the string of hits he masterminded with Richard Rodgers, starting with *Oklahoma!* in the 1940s. Like the straight plays on which they are often based, musical plays generally go in for more serious or at least more thought-provoking subjects than their comedy counterparts, and for more realistic characters and stories as well. But realistic characters in realistic situations are not likely to be caught—*flagrante delicto*—singing. And musical plays, forced to deal with the embarrassment, often "integrate" what makes them *musical* into what makes them *plays*. Thus, a musical play uses songs and dances to move the action of its story forward where a musical comedy might simply dote on them for their own sake, in production numbers designed literally to stop the show.

Candide and *West Side Story*, however, only resembled musical plays. Indeed, what made them such genre-breaking works had to do with a seriousness that seemed to go beyond the ambition of the musical play itself. Though Broadway shows, they thumbed their noses at the working norms of musical comedies *and* musical plays. For one thing, their scripts were not adaptations of more or less modern sources, but were based on centuries-old masterpieces of European literature: *Candide* and *Romeo and Juliet*. Then too, they were written not by behind-the-scenes expert librettists, but by "legitimate" playwrights who, though distinguished indeed, were unaccustomed to the idiosyncrasies of the musical stage: Lillian Hellman (*The Little Foxes*) adapted the Voltaire story and Arthur Laurents (*Home of the Brave*) the Shakespeare. Furthermore, the shows' directors were not exactly of the musical theater. Their credentials were drawn chiefly on accomplishments, however excellent, in other performing arts: Sir Tyrone Guthrie in drama, Jerome Robbins in dance. On it went; and as it did the shows became more and more serious.

If the two shows complemented each other in what was for Broadway outrageous theatrical ambition, in musical ambition they coin-

*Chita Rivera (Anita) and
Carol Lawrence (Maria)
in* West Side Story, *1957*

*An exuberant Bernstein at
the pre-Broadway tryout
of* West Side Story,
Washington, D.C., 1957

cided—in the person of Bernstein himself. The similarities themselves are telling. In several instances, in fact, music intended for one show eventually found its way into the other (*Candide*'s "Oh, Happy We" was originally in *West Side Story*; and *Story*'s "One Hand, One Heart," in *Candide*). More generally, as the two shows were worked on by the same composer at about the same time, the same kinds of musical processes gave shape to both. However sharp their differences in other respects, musically *Candide* and *Story* represent different sides of a single creative coin. Though the one is satirical, it is not without musical moments of sheer grandeur and intensity ("Make Our Garden Grow") that would seem more at home in the other, which, in turn, though of the stuff of melodrama and even tragedy, is not without its musical equivalents in parody and banana-peel humor ("Gee, Officer Krupke").

That both shows ran a similarly disquieting course between the serious and the comedic was a major source of confusion as to what they really were and whether they belonged on Broadway at all. To be sure, musical comedies also had room for tender and even touching songs, but never had they gone in for such emotionally devastating songs as *Candide*'s "Meditations." And musical plays for their part had a place for charming, humorous, and downright funny numbers, but rarely for such scathingly satirical numbers as *Story*'s "America" (the very lyrics of which prompted an irate article in defense of Puerto Rico in the *New York Times*). Considering the expressive straits through which show music was used to steering, the emotional compass of the music in these two works was uncommonly wide, and within that expanse, Bernstein found leeway to mix all sorts of theater-music conventions to arrive at something new.

He carried his preoccupation with "a new form" of American musical from his TV broadcast to the pages of the *New York Times*. Talking of *Candide* just before its Broadway opening, Bernstein said, "The particular mixture of styles and elements that goes into this work makes it perhaps a new kind of show. Maybe it will turn out to be some sort of new form; I don't know. There seems to be no really specific precedent for it in our theater." And as far back as 1949 he had voiced a similar concern when he referred privately to what would become *West Side Story* as "a musical that tells a tragic story in musical-comedy terms, using only musical-comedy techniques, never falling into the 'operatic' trap. Can it succeed? It hasn't yet in our country. I'm excited. If it can work—it's the first."

Marc Blitzstein and Bernstein running through the Brecht/Weill
Three Penny Opera *in Blitzstein's translation prior to its*
production at Brandeis, 1952

Clearly what Bernstein was after was an extraordinary—and seemingly contradictory—goal: something with the power of opera in the medium of musical comedy. His theatrical ambition, then, really had almost nothing to do with musical comedy itself, and more to do with a *musical* play than with any musical *play*. (Loesser, who had similar ambitions for *The Most Happy Fella*, slyly referred to that show as "a musical with music"!) The distinction, even the very terms, were slippery and imprecise. Already at the time of the Broadway premiere of Marc Blitzstein's *Regina*, a musical adaptation of *The Little Foxes*, Bernstein expressed the need for a special

> substitute word which can describe the Broadway
> equivalent of what was once known as opera and which
> excludes the forms we know so well as "musical comedy"
> and "revue". . . . "Musical play" has served nobly and well
> until now, most recently in the case of *South Pacific*;
> but *Regina* is a far more ambitious musical undertaking,
> containing more music, more kinds of music, more
> complicated music, and more unconventional music than
> *South Pacific*.

In describing this work—one he greatly admired—by Blitzstein, a close friend and mentor, Bernstein in effect articulated the musical program for the kind of "musicals with music" he himself would write in the next decade. Substitute *Candide* or *West Side Story* for *Regina*, and the description holds rather well. Take *West Side Story*, for example. It is a show with more music than that of most musical plays: not just the customary dozen or so vocal numbers and scenes, but another half dozen elaborate dance sequences with music of their own. It also has more kinds of music: bebop ("Cool"), vaudeville ("Gee, Officer Krupke"), Latin ("America"), etc. More complicated music: chromatic fugues ("Cool"), sprung rhythms ("Scherzo"), dissonant countermelodies ("A Boy Like That"), etc. And more unconventional music: octatonic scales ("The Rumble"), polymeters ("Tonight Ensemble"), non-thirty-two-bar songs ("Maria"), etc. The description of a "more musical" musical than the music play, as far as it goes, is applicable to Bernstein's own efforts.

Applied to *West Side Story*, however, the description leaves out one thing needed to complete the musical picture of the work, a thing surely at least as important as the ambitiousness of its very undertaking: its success. *West Side Story* was, in fact, an extraordinary work as much because of the way its musical elements were employed as because of the fact of their employment. Its music may have been unconventional in style, but it was nevertheless popular. It may have been complicated in its techniques, but for simple dramatic reasons. It may have taken many different forms of expression, but these came together in a single score. And perhaps it even had too much music altogether for its genre, but much that was essential in the work was still spoken. In sum, *Story* was a work of almost operatic ambition; but it was also a Broadway show, a hit show in fact—and musically all of a piece.

While *Story* broke with the more obvious musical conventions of an acknowledged Broadway style, it was in the Broadway arena— not the opera house—that it chose to test itself, and it was there that it succeeded. Somehow Bernstein was able to filter the plenitude of a "classical" composer's technique and imagination through the musical strictures of Broadway and not have the result come out sounding as if something essential was lost in the process. His was a rare gift indeed, one that must have baffled most of his fellow writers of show music who had no comparable training or musical culture. Those few who had such backgrounds either, like Blitzstein (*The Cradle Will Rock*; *Regina*), did not write commercial hits; or, like Kurt Weill (*Lady in the Dark*; *One Touch of Venus*), did so by suppressing most of the audible signs of fluency in serious musical thought.

By contrast, Bernstein simply let his intimacy with even the grandest of musical utterances rub off on the very compositions with which he made his bid for commercial success. There are similar march-like shapes, for example, in Stravinsky's *Symphony of Psalms* (Ex. 1a) and *West Side Story* (Ex. 1b), each made out of dislocated sonorities of thirds and triads in the melody and a meter-defying pattern of three scale-steps in the bass. But the differences are as striking as the similarities; and what may have begun with an unconventional (and unconscious) source of inspiration for a piece of show music wound up in a more Broadway-accessible form: with fewer angular bass notes and more swinging thirds. (Stravinsky for his part seems to have had no use for Broadway at all, though he did contribute music to a 1944 Billy Rose revue, *The Seven Lively Arts*.)

Yet complicated techniques were also part of *Story*'s musical apparatus—though not for complicated ends. Consider the case of ensembles, those musical numbers involving more than one vocalist. Ensembles have been rare in musical comedies since, by comparison

Ex. 1a: Stravinsky: *Symphony of Psalms* (1930), 3rd movement, mm. 114–123.

Ex. 1b: Bernstein: *West Side Story* (1957), Act I, No. 10, "Tonight Ensemble," mm. 1–9.

with songs, they tend to be more musically developed and more dramatically integrated—and thus less adaptable commercially as single "hits" outside the theater. Songs, in fact, have occupied such a central position in musicals that—even in musical plays—when an ensemble, say a duet, occurs, it often amounts to no more than a song for two: in "People Will Say We're In Love" (from *Oklahoma!*), the two singers take their separate turns singing the same music (though mostly to different words). But what takes place between Anita and Maria in the second act of *West Side Story* is a duet with a musical difference. Here we get a continuous musical scene, two songs, as it were, for the price of one, and both singers singing at the same time. Moreover, it is precisely through such a complication of musical means that the dramatic action of the scene is articulated in its clearest form.

While the situation itself is operatic in the nineteenth-century sense, the music mines a vein of Manhattan *verismo* that Gian Carlo Menotti had explored en route from Bleecker Street to Broadway. In Bernstein's Upper West Side, Anita rages at Maria (the modern Juliet) when she discovers that the girl has been sleeping with Tony (Romeo)—"A Boy Like That" who has "killed your brother" (Ex. 2a). Devastated, Maria can only confess, "I Have a Love," yet she pleads her case in such heartfelt terms that she causes Anita to relent and finally wins her over (Ex. 2b). The complexity with which the two women oppose each other in the first song (rhythms diverge; intervals

Ex. 2a: No. 15, "A Boy Like That/I Have a Love" mm. 44–47

Ex. 2b: mm. 105–109   Andante sostenuto

are dissonant) gives way to the utter simplicity of their coming together in the second (rhythms converge; intervals are consonant). There is an emotional turnaround here on which the rest of the show's plot hinges; and the emotion is brought home in music at least as well as in words. Dialogue has in effect been made music, so that the change in musical texture signals, more palpably than through words, a change in emotional meaning that motivates dramatic action. Rodgers and Hammerstein also used musical scenes to move their plots along, but never did they wage their dramatic arguments on such purely musical terms as this.

Still there is more to the duet than initially meets the ear. The two songs conflict in practically every way: the first expresses the feelings of Anita, who sings *allegro con fuoco* and in the minor (Ex. 3a); the second those of Maria, who sings *andante sostenuto* and in the major (Ex. 3b). For all the differences, however, the essential part of the two melodies is really one and the same: same contour, same phrases, even the identical notes. In the spoken theater Maria would be throwing Anita's own words back at her; here, it is done with pitches. The two songs are thus related by a common musical bond that takes its logic from the continuity of the musical scene in which they both

Ex. 3a: No. 15, "A Boy Like That/I Have a Love" mm. 18–20

Ex. 3b: mm. 68–72

appear. That kind of bonding offers a glimpse into a larger compositional process characteristic of Bernstein and aimed at linking not just two songs, but the whole variety of separate musical numbers throughout the show.

West Side Story contains many different kinds of music from start to finish, yet these are held together by a very special sense of belonging to a single musical score. A score is more than just the sum of all the notes in a show. A score gives a sense of unity to the music much as a story line unifies the book. Songs and other musical numbers may help the story along—may even become indispensable to the telling of it—but of itself, the sheer accumulation of songs does not add up to a score. What may be missing is a certain texture to the music, a pervasive quality to the sound such that, while each song differs from the next, it also has some kind of special connection to it. Presumably because that sound is unique to each show, Richard Rodgers liked to think of it as a "family resemblance."

Opera composers have traditionally commanded all sorts of means for making a word sound in that family way, from the choice of particular keys (like *The Magic Flute*'s E-flat) to the very colors of the orchestra (like *The Magic Flute*'s trombones, associated with church music in Mozart's day). But on Broadway, keys have been the choice less of composers than of performers (who are most comfortable singing in a certain range); and orchestrations again the choice less of composers than of one or another of the behind-the-scenes specialists (arrangers, orchestrators, etc.) to whom Bernstein refers as "those subcomposers who turn a series of songs into a unified score, who make it all sound like a 'work'." For Bernstein, the composer of what might be considered "a series of songs," also to have written his own arrangements and to have had a major hand in determining his own orchestrations is unusual on Broadway. Beyond that departure, what has made his theater scores most particularly sound like "works" is something that inheres in their very composition: his choice of a unifying musical interval—the perfect fourth (and by extension, the minor seventh or major second) in *Candide*, and in *West Side Story*, the tritone.

Often held to be the single most disruptive element in traditional music, the tritone is used as the simplest sound to embody the underlying tension that makes for *Story*'s story. With astonishing invention Bernstein allows it to color the entire score, and it works its way tellingly into all the musical textures. The tritone puts an awk-

West Side Story Tritones

Ex. 4a: No. 8, "Cool"

Ex. 4b: No. 5, "Maria"

Ex. 4c: 6 & 10, "Tonight"

Ex. 4d: No. 17, "Finale"

ward edge on a melody in "Cool" (Ex. 4a). It undoes the traditional harmonies between the bass and the top of a chord in "Maria" (Ex. 4b), the middle of a chord in "Tonight" (Ex. 4c), and the bottom of a chord in the "Finale" (Ex. 4d). It provides a nervous framework for a harmonic progression in "Tonight" (Ex. 4e). And it haunts the counterpoint of fugue-like entries along an "octatonic" scale (C-D♭-E♭-E-F♯-G-A-B♭-C) in "The Rumble" (Ex. 4f). As the quintessential sound that provides the unifying sense of a score in the work, the tritone seems to be everywhere. Giving irrefutable evidence of the intelligence of a compositional mind at work, it pursues the star-crossed lovers—pursues them musically, that is, up to a certain point. For the kind of control a composer normally exercises at every step en route to a musical composition can only be made to work at a local level on Broadway. The bigger the decisions in the making of a show, the more a composer's self-criticism has to give way to external constraints, constraints that are powerful enough at times to silence his voice altogether.

Thus, when the sheer quantity of *Story*'s music—vocal, symphonic, balletic—threatened to dwarf the import of spoken dialogue that

Ex. 4e: No. 6, "Tonight"

Ex. 4f: Nos. 1 & 11, "Prologue" & "The Rumble"

kept the work in touch with the Broadway tradition, some of it had to go. Bernstein's contribution, after all, was only one part in a collaborative effort "to tread the fine line between opera and Broadway," and he simply had to cut back on music or even yield to speech when, as an opera composer, he would have let music take over and soar. The balcony scene, for example, was a twelve-minute musical sequence that had to be cut to seven minutes for theatrical reasons. "That was probably the correct decision, because the dialogue was redundant," recalled Larry Kert, who created the role of Tony, "but a lot of gorgeous music was lost." And music written for the end of the show had to be dropped entirely when it became apparent that—after several tries at a "mad aria" for Maria, gun in hand beside Tony's body—the moment was truer to the kind of work *West Side Story* was with no aria at all. So at the dramatic climax of the musical, Maria now simply speaks where under other circumstances she might have tried to move us with song.

For all the musical ambition of it, then, *Story* was not the opera Arthur Laurents initially feared it might turn into if Bernstein had his way. (To hear the original-cast Columbia recording next to the recent Deutsche Grammophon version—in which, at least as far as performance is concerned, Bernstein finally has his way—is proof enough.) What kind of work was it then, and what was all the fuss really about? It was not Bernstein, but Jerome Robbins who came closest to telling us when, years later, he admitted,

> I wanted to find out at the time how far we, as "long-haired artists," could go in bringing our crafts and talents to a musical. Why did we have to do it separately and elsewhere? Why did Lenny have to write an opera, Arthur a play, me a ballet? Why couldn't we, in aspiration, try to bring our deepest talents together to the commercial theater in this work? That was the true *gesture* of the show.

So together, on Broadway, these artists created what was neither play nor opera nor ballet, but a performance amalgam: a libretto that was one of the shortest ever written for a "book" show because it delegated much if not most of its story-telling authority to music (song) and movement (dance).

But that was what Hammerstein had been up to all along. And when it came to making *West Side Story*, in fact, Hammerstein's advice was both sought (by way of a special run-through, staged for him before out-of-town tryouts) and followed (when he suggested revisions, as he did, for instance, in the balcony scene). It is no surprise that *Story* turned out to be a musical play, then; only it was *the* musical play, which took Hammerstein's notion about as far as it would go, to the culmination of a tradition stemming directly from *Oklahoma!*

It was also something more—and more pretentious. Though the work was transposed to a twentieth-century urban setting and tamed by the ethos of American liberalism, there was a strangely "Wagnerian" aura about the whole thing. What with Bernstein's faith in the linear progress of musical comedy, Laurents's in the mythological hold of his literary source, and Robbins's in the commercial prospect of merging all the arts involved, *West Side Story* took on the trappings of a middle-class *Gesamtkunstwerk*.

There were also traces of Wagnerism in the factitiousness of appealing to history (and Mozart and *The Magic Flute*) to bolster present claims. Now if *West Side Story*, even more than *Candide*, represented something serious that had grown out of a native tradition of popular music and comedy, then it did seem to bear comparison with *The Magic Flute*. But Mozart's *Singspiel* was an *opera*—and not just on account of its more stylized use of instrumental and vocal means. Where Bernstein took an artistically naive form of entertainment to make a musical statement that was as highly sophisticated as it was deeply passionate, Mozart made of the artistically naive something utterly profound. As a *Singspiel*, *The Magic Flute* had its spoken dialogue, its low comedy, its Viennese equivalent of pop tunes, to be sure; but as an opera, it also had, as Shaw said, the only music yet written fit for the mouth of God.

Moreover, if *Story* was some sort of new form, it was also one of a kind. Chiefly through the impact of the work of Robbins, it influenced the Broadway musical in various ways. But it did not turn the genre itself around. (In the decades since, Broadway has become more grandiose, perhaps, but no grander.) Nor did it lead to a new school of American vernacular opera, as Bernstein had hoped it would, though its success at the time, he later said, "led me to believe we were on the way. I say 'we' advisedly, because I felt there would then be a whole succession of young composers who would take the next step, and the next. This, to my regret, has not really happened. The big exception is Stephen Sondheim." And so it is; though Sondheim's work is of a different sensibility altogether, impinging as it does on the world of "postmodernism," and he himself is reputed to have little sympathy for things Mozartean *or* operatic. (If his is indeed "the next step," then historians may come to see as no accident that Sondheim's professional career effectively began in writing the lyrics for *West Side Story*). Virtually nothing else of consequence has come of Broadway's Mozartean moment. And yet, perhaps nothing of Broadway origin, before or since, has ever come as close to speaking on Mozart's terms as Bernstein's twin scores of that moment: *Candide*, in the sparkle of its musical humor, *West Side Story*, in the intensity of its musical passion.

If it seems that way to us now, however, it was not always so. Not often is music of strong intelligence and feeling embraced for what it is right from the start—and especially not where so many other things compete for attention as in the musical theater. On first hearing *The Abduction from the Seraglio*, for example, Emperor Joseph II of Austria is supposed to have remarked to the composer, "Too beautiful for our ears, and far too many notes, my dear Mozart." To this Mozart is said to have replied, "Exactly as many as are needed, Your Majesty." Now, patronage in the performing arts has changed considerably since then, though not much else seems to have changed along with it. And so one can well imagine the thoughts of another theater composer in 1957, the day when representatives of Columbia Records first heard him at the piano auditioning his latest score for an updated version of Shakespeare's *Romeo and Juliet*. "Too depressing," they said, and "too many tritones." And Columbia Records at first turned the work down.

Bernstein at seventy is fortunate to be able to see his grandest "musical comedies" vindicated. Possessed as they are (much like the man himself) of a seemingly inexhaustible fund of vitality, they remain: still performed, yet splendidly embedded in American cultural history.

Liturgy on Stage: Bernstein's Mass

by PAUL HUME

IT was the eighth of September, 1971; the first music to be publicly performed in the Kennedy Center for the Performing Arts was about to begin. The performance was to take place in the Opera House of the center, a gloriously red theater with a blazing chandelier given by the Austrian government. To peer into the future of this opera theater, let me tell you what the late, great conductor Karl Böhm said to me during the weeks when he was conducting the *Deutsche Oper* in the Kennedy Center during our 1976 Bicentennial celebrations: "It is the finest room for music in the world after the *Grosse Musikvereinssaal* in Vienna," was Böhm's authoritative view.

Leonard Bernstein knows as well as anyone in the world the magnificent qualities of the great home of the Vienna Philharmonic. But on that September night, seventeen years ago, no one knew how music would sound in the Kennedy Center Opera House, with every one of its twenty-two hundred seats full, and its unfamiliar acoustical properties still to be tested.

Far more important, no one knew what this new work by Leonard Bernstein was going to be. "Mass—A Theatre Piece. . ." had been written at the request of Jacqueline Kennedy. She had asked him for a new work to dedicate this new Center for the Performing Arts, named in honor of her late husband. But she had not asked Bernstein to write a Mass. The work, unlike anything that Bernstein—or anyone else—has written, came into existence as a logical sequel to his three symphonies: *Jeremiah*, *The Age of Anxiety*, and *Kaddish*. Each of these is concerned with the crisis of faith in our times, a crisis that

As music critic of the *Washington Post*, Paul Hume covered the world premiere of Bernstein's *Mass* in a front-page story.

the composer himself has often discussed in talking about these works. Leonard Bernstein's *Mass* came into being because of this concern and because of his long-time fascination with the idea of writing a setting of the Roman Catholic Mass, every great setting of which by Mozart, Haydn, Beethoven—and their parallels in the Requiems of Berlioz and Verdi—Bernstein has known intimately and conducted. The Bernstein *Mass* also arose in some part out of the composer's fascination with Roman Catholicism and with one of its most dramatic pontiffs, Pope John XXIII.

What is this crisis of faith, of which Bernstein has so often spoken? In 1977, in a Berlin press conference, he said:

> The work I have been writing all my life is about the struggle that is born of the crisis of our century, a crisis of faith. Even way back, when I wrote *Jeremiah*, I was wrestling with that problem.
>
> The faith or peace that is found at the end of *Jeremiah* is really more a kind of comfort, not a solution. Comfort is one way of achieving peace, but it does not achieve the sense of a new beginning, as does the end of *Age of Anxiety* or *Mass*.

By that memorable September in 1971, not only had John Kennedy been assassinated, but—tragically, almost beyond belief—so had his brother, Robert. And so, too, Martin Luther King, Jr. By that autumn, a restlessness of unprecedented proportions had flooded the campuses of the universities and colleges of this country. It was impossible to walk down the halls of some of the major universities without being overwhelmed by the odors of the drugs that had moved in. Where students had, for generations, obeyed the canons of wearing coats and ties to class, cutoffs, jeans, and bare feet had taken over. And the crisis was not confined to the scholastic world.

In churches of many denominations, where, as long as anyone could remember, the music on Sunday mornings had been presented by organists and choirs—made up of volunteer or paid singers—guitars appeared, singly or up to as many as six, eight, and ten at a time. And a music richly inspired and appropriate for every season of the religious year was often unceremoniously shoved out the front door as rectors, ministers, and priests told their musicians, "We are going to have a new kind of music."

At the time that Bernstein began thinking about the work that he would write for the opening of the Kennedy Center, there was, indeed, a crisis—of faith, of religious practices, of public behavior, and of social, philosophical, and religious thought—that no one could ignore. Certainly not the creative genius that was Leonard Bernstein, about to create a new work that would, as inevitably as its predecessors, reflect his most profound concerns.

* * *

If you listen to the dissonance with which Beethoven opens the very first of his nine symphonies, then you will not be demolished by the horrendous chord with which he begins the last movement of his last symphony, the Ninth.

And if you listen to Leonard Bernstein's first symphony, *Jeremiah*, and then listen to his second, *The Age of Anxiety*, and after that give your close attention to his third symphony, *Kaddish*, then you will find it difficult to ask some of the questions that might otherwise press upon you as you listen to his *Mass*.

A similar point was made by William Schuman in 1962 before an assemblage of the country's music critics, who had elected to hold their annual meeting in New York to be on hand for the opening of Philharmonic Hall, the first component of Lincoln Center; it was for this event that Schuman wrote his Eighth Symphony. The composer, who had already served with the utmost distinction as head of the Juilliard School of Music and had become the head of the entire Lincoln Center complex, gave the critics one of the most penetrating talks that organization had ever heard. During the course of his remarks, Schuman said, "I am not speaking to you as the head of the Juilliard School of Music, or as the head of the Lincoln Center. Rather, I am speaking to you as an American composer. And I want to say to you that you have no business discussing or writing about my latest symphony unless you know those that preceded it."

Now just stop for a moment and ponder that remark. What Schuman was saying was that the violent dissonance at the outset of the last movement of Beethoven's Ninth Symphony was clearly foreshadowed by the dissonant opening of his First; that Gustav Mahler's Ninth Symphony is the legitimate and direct descendant of his First Symphony.

* * *

Leonard Bernstein put the same thought this way: "In a sense, I suppose, I am always writing the same piece, as all composers do. But each time it is a new attempt in other terms to write *this* piece, to have a piece achieve new dimensions, or even acquire a new vocabulary. The work I have been writing all my life is about the struggle that is born of the crisis of our century, a crisis of faith."

Nowhere—not even in his much more recent opera, *A Quiet Place*—is that crisis so dramatically and so forcefully laid out for an audience as in *Mass*. Remember its descriptive title, "A Theatre Piece." That word "theatre" is central to all of Bernstein's musical thought. He said, when *The Age of Anxiety* was new, "I have a deep suspicion that every work I write, for whatever medium, is really theater music in some way." There is, however, no conflict between the ideas of the Mass and the framework of the theater. Some of Roman Catholicism's finest practitioners have described the ritual of the Mass as the greatest theater in the world.

The outcry that greeted the Bernstein *Mass* after its premiere in the Kennedy Center arose, I have often thought, from two segments of the critical public and, perhaps to a lesser extent, of the general public as well: first, from those who failed—or refused—to see what Bernstein was saying and why he said it in the ways he did; and second, from those who—to recall William Schuman's adjuration to the music critics—did not know Bernstein's *Jeremiah*, his *Age of Anxiety*, and his *Kaddish*.

For more than thirty years the celebration of the Roman Catholic Mass has been changing in its appearance, in its language, and in the music often heard during its performance. It was in 1957 that the custom, now widely observed, of having the Celebrant say the Mass while facing the people, rather than with his back to them, began to be introduced into this country. The archbishop of Washington at that time forbade the new idea, but the Jesuits of Georgetown University simply exercised their prerogative of deciding how they would celebrate Mass on their own territory and continued to employ the new format.

Early in the 1970s an organist in Charlotte, North Carolina, who had served an Episcopal church long and faithfully, providing both organ and choral music of a high caliber week after week, was told summarily by the rector of that parish that her services would not be needed after the end of the month. The liturgy would be accompanied by guitar.

No—the collapse of the sacred liturgy that comes about during the course of Leonard Bernstein's *Mass* is not something woven by the composer and his brilliant theatrical associate Stephen Schwartz out of some cloth that had no precedent in the liturgical worlds of its time. Rather, it is a clear mirror of much that was most disturbing in some parishes in those days, and at the same time it is an exploration of the crisis to which Bernstein so often refers: a crisis of faith—of one kind in *Jeremiah*, of another in *The Age of Anxiety*, and of still another in *Kaddish*.

I once asked Bernstein about the angry outbreak in the second movement of *Kaddish*, in which the Speaker bursts out angrily against God Himself. "Ah," he answered me, "but you see, you don't realize that Jews often talk to God that way. They are allowed to."

And so it is in *Mass*, when the Celebrant, exhausted and no longer able to stand the outbursts of his people, reaches a frenzy of total madness in which he questions everything in which he has ever believed: his congregation, their behavior, the liturgy, his own personal God. And only when he has finally found some inner way to peace and a chance that he can try once again to make it all work does he find even an infinitesimal degree of hope.

And all of this Bernstein achieves—as does every great composer—through his music. His *Mass* opens with four voices on tape, electronically singing the *Kyrie eleison*, purposely assailing our ears from all four corners of the theater. Suddenly, at the height of the madly confused singing, a single chord on a guitar stops the taped voice, and the Celebrant, wearing blue jeans and playing his guitar, sings one of Bernstein's most inspired melodies, *A Simple Song*.

From that point on, every word of the Catholic Mass is sung, interspersed with the contemporary text that reflects the growing discontent, disbelief, unhappiness, and dissatisfaction of the congregation until they are shouting for a peace that "won't keep on breaking." The frenzy mounts until, with his congregation in complete disarray and misconduct, the Celebrant hurls the sacraments to the floor—an act that stops his congregation in its tracks while he makes his agonized way through his own disbelief and uncertainty, finally emerging as if to try once more for a new hope.

Giuseppe Verdi was accused of writing far too theatrically—too operatically—in his setting of the Requiem Mass, while Hector Berlioz was accused of even more violent crimes in his setting of the same text. Leonard Bernstein has made very clear his reasons for calling *Mass* "A Theatre Piece." Every time the liturgy of the Roman Catholic Mass is performed, it is a matter, in part, of theater. Bernstein and Schwartz have given the ancient text a new dimension and placed it in a context that illuminates it in an age when belief is not easy and faith is seeking new as well as old foundations.

Lord of the Dance:
Bernstein's Concert Music

by STEVEN LEDBETTER

DAVID leaped and danced before the ark of the Lord, even though by doing so he incurred the contempt of Saul's daughter Michal, who evidently found his behavior unseemly. Leonard Bernstein, a latter-day David, leaps and dances, too, in the unlikely venue of the concert hall. I am not referring to his familiar athleticism on the podium, but rather to his music. For the force that animates Bernstein's music seems, in the first instance, to be rhythm, particularly as conceived in those exhilarating, quickening patterns that engender the dance.

It should be no surprise that two of his earliest large works were ballet scores, *Fancy Free* (1944) and *Facsimile* (1946), or that his Broadway shows should have unusually elaborate dance numbers that he himself composed (contrary to the normal Broadway tradition, in which the dance sequences are relegated to an assistant). Even more telling is the fact that dance sequences from two of his shows, *On the Town* and *West Side Story*, have made their way into the concert hall, for in complexity and craft they go far beyond a tinkly rhythmicized background for a soft-shoe routine or the kicking of chorus girls, to reach a level of interest found in the work of only a few other masters whose music for the dance has also attracted the attention of concert-goers.

Prior to becoming the Boston Symphony Orchestra's musicologist and program annotator in 1979, Steven Ledbetter taught at New York University and Dartmouth College. He is an editor of critical editions of the music of the Italian madrigalist Luca Marenzio and of the comic operas of Gilbert and Sullivan. In recent years he has studied the development of American music for orchestra, especially as exemplified by the Boston school of composers at the turn of the century.

Ballet was, of course, a central component of the work of one of Bernstein's principal sources of inspiration, Igor Stravinsky, and it played a considerable part in the career of another figure, Aaron Copland, who strongly influenced him.

It is striking that, having begun so auspiciously in the ballet, Bernstein did not choose to continue in that line, for (with the exception of dance sequences for Broadway) there is not another ballet until *The Dybbuk* (1974), and he has composed none since then. Yet it is not so surprising, perhaps, if we consider how thoroughly imbued with the spirit of the dance is his work as a whole. Bernstein has not needed the prospect of actual physical dancers to spark his rhythmic imagination, whether in the symphonies or in other works performed on the concert stage. And since the vivid theatricality of his music, with its variety and rhythmic energy, does not fit easily into the pigeonholes that we normally set up for the concepts "symphony" or "concerto" or even "concert music," the dancing quality of this latter-day David's music has perhaps tended to arouse the contempt of concert-going Michals.

Two cautionary points need to be made at once:

First, when I refer to "dance music" or to a balletic quality, I am not speaking of the nondescript stuff turned out in reams by nineteenth-century ballet masters for productions designed more to show off the ballerinas' legs than to create an artistically satisfying synthesis of music and movement. Music of that sort is wearyingly predictable from its first bars. The listener knows that every phrase is going to be repeated (to allow the dancer to perform a step first to the right, then to the left); the phrases are so easily anticipated time and time again that the music quickly becomes exasperating.

But no one would accuse Bernstein's dance music—even that written explicitly for the ballet—of "oom-pah-pah" simplicity. It shares, along with the scores of such great masters of the dance as Tchaikovsky, Stravinsky, and Copland, a greater textural complexity and variety and greater interest in large-scale musical shaping, which, for lack of a better word, I will call "symphonic." (In using the word, I have history on my side: it was the term applied in the nineteenth century—though usually in disapproval—to works like the ballets of Delibes and Tchaikovsky; since the symphony was then generally regarded as the highest level to which musical art could aspire, "symphonic," as applied to the ballet, suggested that this form of entertainment was getting a little high-falutin', aiming beyond its

Stravinsky and Bernstein backstage at the New York City Center after Bernstein had conducted the New York City Symphony Orchestra in the Symphony of Psalms, *January 21, 1946*

rightful place in the scheme of things.) As I use the phrase "dance music" here, I am speaking simply of music that has a gestural quality implying stylized physical movement, if not in fact compelling it.

Second, I am not by any means asserting that Bernstein's music has no qualities *other* than the balletic; I wish simply to draw attention to the frequency and ease with which he brings gestural elements into musical scores even in "abstract" genres. In this respect, Bernstein's work is especially linked to that of his great models Stravinsky and Copland.

At the same time, the balletic element is intertwined with all of his other musical and cultural concerns. In his symphonies, for example, progressing to the theatrical *Mass*, Bernstein is concerned with issues of faith and its crisis in the modern world. That concern can be reflected in inspiration from the Bible, from an Auden poem about modern life, or from a traditional Jewish prayer. And, as Jack Gottlieb has shown (in the *Musical Quarterly* for April 1980), many of the thematic motifs in these works play a symbolic as well as a musical role.

Symbolism can occur in the harmony as well—especially in the interplay between clearly tonal sections and passages in which the sense of tonal center is, at the very least, clouded, and even thoroughly negated by twelve-tone technique. Bernstein's career as a composer has paralleled the development, the spread, and the wide acceptance (among composers, if not among the concert-going audience) of Schoenbergian twelve-tone technique as the predominant approach. So strongly was this development entrenched, especially in academic centers of musical study during the 1950s and '60s, that those composers who chose to follow a different path were relegated to the peripheries of musical life and branded "conservative" or "regressive." During that period Bernstein's music was heard and discussed far more than the work of many of his contemporaries who remained tonally oriented largely because he was also one of the leading conductors of the day and was thus constantly in the spotlight; he could, at the very least, guarantee a hearing for his works by programming them himself.

A composer as curious and intense in his musical interests as Leonard Bernstein would not, of course, dismiss the twelve-tone technique out of hand, and, indeed, he made serious attempts to write in the "current" style, especially during a sabbatical year from conducting at the New York Philharmonic in the mid-1960s. But he threw out almost everything he had written then on the grounds that it was not honest music, not *his* music, and returned with full commitment to tonality, though this return meant, inevitably, facing criticism and ridicule from the avant-garde.

Still, his skirmish with twelve-tone music—as well as his experience of conducting many of the major compositions written in that style, such as the works of Berg, which he has found particularly sympathetic—left its mark on his music as well. Serial or twelve-tone elements appear in Bernstein's work far more often than one might imagine from his reputation as a "conservative" composer—and they appear in places where one would not have guessed that an audience might accept them. On Broadway, for example: the instrumental fugue embedded in the song "Cool" in *West Side Story* has a twelve-tone theme, a complete tone-row. And in *Songfest*, Bernstein's Bicentennial tribute to the minorities, the outcasts, and the forgotten people of American history, the setting of Lawrence Ferlinghetti's "The Pennycandystore Beyond the El" is consistently twelve-tone throughout, and comes across sounding like cool jazz.

For the most part twelve-tone sections occur within a larger, fundamentally tonal, framework. They function as large areas of instability, set off ultimately from the stabilizing character of a tonal center, which Bernstein feels strongly as basic to music and to the natural human perception of music (a feeling he argued passionately in his Norton lectures at Harvard, published as *The Unanswered Question*). Probably the work that plays most explicitly on the structural basis of tonal-against-atonal is *Halil* (1981), for solo flute and small orchestra. Composed in memory of a young Israeli flautist killed in the 1973 war, it is, as the composer wrote in his program note, "a kind of night music . . . an ongoing conflict of nocturnal images," from nightmares to reposeful dreams. The harmonic style shifts rapidly, sometimes between one phrase and another, from intense non-tonal dissonance to calm major-key harmonies. As so often in Bernstein's music, the opposition of styles is dramatically conceived and essentially programmatic.

The interaction among these diverse harmonic elements takes place most immediately on the level of the thematic motif. Though Bernstein—far more than most living composers—has written memorable melodies, his thematic shapes do not, for the most part, appear complete and whole in a single burst. Rather, they grow from tiny atoms of three or four notes, repeated, expanded, inverted, elaborated—springboards for the melodic line. This evolution makes possible a link between strikingly different musical styles with the motif embedded, in each case, within different harmonic worlds.

One other important element in Bernstein's music needs to be discussed here—and it is one that will bring us back, finally, to the subject of the dance. Few composers of our time have been more willing to be eclectic. It takes a certain courage to do so, since the very word has been practically an obscenity in some musical circles. How can a composer claim that he is serious at his work, some have asked, if he openly borrows stylistic elements from hither and yon, particularly from the world of jazz or popular commercial music? Surely it is the business of a composer to create his own style, free of "taint" from any outside source? Yes, of course, one may be "influenced" by a teacher, say, or a great historic precedent. But what can be made of a composer whose work shows the influences of Mahler, Stravinsky, Harold Arlen, Louis Armstrong, Hebrew liturgical cantillation, and John Lennon, all rolled into one?

The argument arises in part out of what seems to me a historical misconception. Few composers, including some of the greatest, have failed to be "eclectic." J. S. Bach learned a great deal about rhythmic drive and dramatic energy from Vivaldi's music, while drawing upon his own Protestant German tradition of hymn tunes and contrapuntal technique or even, occasionally, on suggestions of folk song. Mozart, who had traveled and heard music all over Europe while still a child, was a great musical sponge, absorbing everything he heard and sending it back into the world transformed. Handel, too, brought together elements gathered from Italy and Germany, France and England, in his own personal fusion.

Composers have always learned from their teachers and from the music around them. American composers, though, are in a unique situation: just as the history of this country is the story of people coming from somewhere else to make a new life alongside of immigrants from a different place, the story of America's music is the history of many different strands brought from all over the world and joined into new combinations. The twentieth century in particular, with its speedy travel and instantaneous communication, has broken down—or at least minimized—most of the cultural enclaves that formerly could remain private musical worlds, with very little music passing in or out from other sources. Where a Mozart might absorb fewer than a half-dozen musical traditions, the contemporary American musician has access to a whole world of ethnic musical traditions, a thriving and enormously varied range of popular music, and the entire history of Western European art music.

As perhaps the quintessential American musician, Bernstein has embraced this world wholeheartedly, has accepted the view that music is a universal part of human life, and that the music of one section of the human family can speak directly to another. He has, therefore, been utterly unabashed in drawing on an extraordinarily wide range of "influences" in his own work, many of them dance rhythms or patterns.

The impulse of a regular beat sets the feet going, or the hands, and has an effect on breathing and pulse as well. Most historical dances, at least most of the dances widely known in the European tradition, have been based on simple duple or triple meters, repeating for a considerable period some variation on

ONE–two, ONE–two, ONE–two

or

ONE–two–three, ONE–two–three, ONE–two–three.

Needless to say, many such rhythmically stirring dance patterns are to be found in Bernstein's music. But what is most characteristic of him is an asymmetrical pattern, like a five- or seven-beat figure, which is normally composed of some combination of the basic duple or triple meters.

No doubt, one of the things that interests him in these asymmetrical patterns is their inherent ambiguity. Is a five-pattern to be understood as 2+3 or as 3+2? It can be either, of course. And it can be more than that: I remember a class in the conducting seminar at Tanglewood in 1986, when Bernstein had just come from a rehearsal of Tchaikovsky's *Pathétique* Symphony with the Boston Symphony Orchestra. That symphony, Tchaikovsky's last work, has a striking second movement in 5/4 time, perhaps the earliest consistent use of quintuple meter. When the symphony was first performed in Vienna, the senior critic there, the conservative Eduard Hanslick, declared the rhythm to be "barbaric" and opined that it would consign Tchaikovsky's symphony to speedy oblivion. Bernstein, on the other hand, reveled in the 5/4 meter precisely because Tchaikovsky played so elegantly with the alternation of 2+3 and 3+2; setting up both patterns simultaneously in different sections of the orchestra, he generated a feeling of lightness, a "lift," throughout the work.

I am tempted to declare that Bernstein's own fundamental rhythmic gesture is the still more complex 7/4, which can be parsed as 2+2+3 or 3+2+2 or even 2+3+2. And what comes as a constant, delightful surprise in his treatment of this septuple rhythm—which would seem to be even more "barbaric" than Tchaikovsky's 5/4—is its utter naturalness. I remember being astonished to discover, when first hearing the original cast album of *Candide* in the late 1950s, a passage in the overture (which later turns up in the show as "Oh Happy We") written in a septuple pattern of 2+2+3. But what delighted me most about the discovery was not the simple fact that the melody went in sevens, but that it sounded so right!

How many choral singers have learned, to their astonishment, that a "difficult" septuple meter is enormously invigorating to sing when they essay the *Chichester Psalms*? Here the pattern of 2+2+3 goes by so fast that the performer feels it as a kind of triple meter with a little extra delay on the last beat: ONE-and-TWO-and-THREE-and-a, ONE-and-TWO-and-THREE-and-a . . .

The conversion of a seven-beat pattern to a kind of triple meter is made explicit in the *Divertimento*, where "Waltz" is not in the expected 3/4 time, but in 7/8, parsed 3+2+2. Here Bernstein gives a particular lilt to his waltz—though the lilt is American, not Viennese—by making the first waltz beat in each bar half again as long as the second and third: ONE-and-a-TWO-and-THREE-and, ONE-and-a-TWO-and-THREE-and . . .

Of course, he uses many other dance patterns as well, sometimes explicit, sometimes only implied. The *Divertimento*, as its title suggests, is a piece to have fun with, and like the divertimentos of Classical composers, it is made up largely of movements in dance patterns. Bernstein's choices of dance, though, are distinctly those of a modern American composer, drawing from a large international repertory of styles that have had an impact here: waltz, mazurka, samba, and turkey trot among them.

I referred earlier to dance music, as in the ballet, that might be called "symphonic." It would perhaps be unusual, but not incorrect I think, to refer to Bernstein's symphonies as being, in some way, balletic. Not, of course, that they are intended to be danced to—though several have been choreographed. But they involve elements of the dance, or of gestural music, within large-scale, multi-movement, abstract works.

His three "symphonies" are entitled, respectively, *Jeremiah* (1942), *The Age of Anxiety* (1949), and *Kaddish* (1963). As these headings alone may suggest, not one of them is a symphony in the classical sense of the word, though they fit the genre well enough in an extended Mahlerian sense (which is surely the appopriate sense to consider when speaking of music composed by one of the great devotees of Mahler). All of them are programmatic; two of them add the human voice, and a text, to the resources of the orchestra. And all three of them make extensive use of gestural music.

Jeremiah, which contains some of the earliest music by Bernstein that we are likely to hear in a concert (parts of it were composed in the late 1930s), consists of three movements with the titles "Prophecy," "Profanation," "Lamentation," the last bringing in a mezzo-soprano to sing, in Hebrew, a passage from the Lamentations of Jeremiah. The first and last movements are in relatively slow tempos, the second a *Vivace con brio* that is the most gestural part of the work. It is a driving, dynamic movement with a steady eighth-note pulse, but the eighth-notes are grouped in various ways—mostly 6/8, 8/8 (parsed 2+3+3), and 7/8—and the constant shifting from one to another of these meters lends a nervous quality to the music. This is in no way a dance of joy in life, rather its opposite—a grim dance of joy in destruction, in the profaning of that which is sacred. In the midst of this dance of destruction, a prominent motive from the first movement—Jeremiah's prophecy—in the bottom and top of the orchestra recalls that prophecy come true.

W. H. Auden's eclogue *The Age of Anxiety* provided far more than a title for Bernstein's Second Symphony: it provided what must be called the plot. The composer's note in the published score describes his astonishment at realizing, after the fact, how closely the music echoed the poem, which had been intended as no more than a general guide to its structure and expression. This detailed rendering of a poetic text into music has, perhaps, been a stumbling block to listeners. Certainly anyone who, like me, encountered the symphony prior to reading Auden and used the composer's elaborate program note as a guide, was probably irritated at the wordy description, which seemed to obstruct rather than illuminate the music. Not a few composers have written extended programmatic descriptions as an aid to the audience only to find that, for most listeners, the music alone says its piece far better than words could do. Bernstein himself had second thoughts about so literal an attempt at mirroring words in music, at least to the extent of rewriting the epilogue so that the piano soloist—who, in the original version, drops out entirely except for a final chord—now has the normal musical function in a concerto-like work, playing against the orchestral ensemble. (I must add, though, that *after* learning the music and reading Auden's poem, it is fascinating to compare the two, using Bernstein's program note as a beacon.)

Nonetheless, the "narrative" of *The Age of Anxiety* is projected effectively in the music itself, and especially in the contrasting rhythmic patterns, which often hint at specific dances. The first half of Bernstein's score, after a prologue, consists of two sets of seven variations each, "The Seven Ages," and "The Seven Stages." These are not "variations on a theme" in the traditional sense, but fourteen short, contrasting sections each of which grows out of some musical idea in the preceding passage and generates another idea that will lead to what follows.

The rhythms through much of the symphony mirror the nervousness and hectic pace of modern urban life. But a striking exception is Variation VIII, the first of the "Seven Stages." The poem speaks of darkness and of a feeling of remoteness, and hints at distant times and places. Bernstein casts the music of this section in a broad 3/2 with a flowing melody in quarters and eighths over a stately bass line moving in half notes. It is almost impossible to avoid hearing, in this passage, the echo of a "remote" dance style from the distant time and place, the sarabande so common in the Baroque suite. At the other end of the tempo spectrum is the liveliest component of the Baroque suite, the gigue—or, to put it in plain English, the jig— which makes a joyous appearance in the last movement of the Serenade for solo violin, string orchestra, harp, and percussion.

Bernstein's Third Symphony, *Kaddish*, is the most extreme case among his concert works (*Mass* being, of course, a theater piece) of the search for a lost or problematic faith. The Hebrew (actually, Aramaic) text that is set three times in the course of the piece for the chorus and soprano soloist is the prayer chanted for the dead, a connotation that might naturally give rise to questions of ultimate concern. But the *Kaddish* text is an affirmation of life and expresses praise to God throughout. In the symphony, doubts arise in the words of a speaker who, uttering the composer's own English text, talks back to God, sometimes in praise or supplication, but often in aggressive complaint (rather in the manner of Job). The interplay between the speaker (who, in the revised score of the symphony, is always accompanied by music) and the chorus provides the dramatic design of the work.

Though the musical progress of *Kaddish* traces a wide arc through traditional, popular, folkloric, jazz, and twelve-tone styles, the most striking feature of the work—especially in the choral part—is its extraordinary quality of physicality. The first choral entrance begins with a hushed treatment of the opening words of the *Kaddish* followed by a joyous explosion (the score is marked "Wild!") of 7/8 time alternating with 3/4. The 7/8 measure consists of three beats, of which the first is slightly longer (3 + 2 + 2 eighth-notes), and the

The Age of Anxiety: (top left) *poet W. H. Auden, whose eclogue inspired the score, discussing it with Bernstein (January 23, 1950).* (Bottom left) *after the Tanglewood performance of August 11, 1949, a proud Koussevitzky shakes the hand of his protégé, who was both composer and soloist.* (Below) *Bernstein analyzes the score for a class of Tanglewood auditors, August 1949 (conductor Artur Rodzinski is sitting in).*

3/4 measure also consists of three beats, but even ones (2+2+2). The effect is of a wonderfully enthusiastic waltz, slightly skewed through the weight given to the downbeat of every other measure.

Soon after, another expression of praise evokes physical movement from the singers: while altos and basses sing the words, sopranos and tenors are required to clap the rhythm of another uneven triple meter, this one based on 8/8 time, divided into 3+2+3 eighth-notes. It is as near as concert performers can get to actually dancing!

This opening portion is lively and energetic; "*Kaddish* II," featuring the soprano soloist, is a gentle 5/8 lullaby with a middle section at twice the speed. Here again, whether tender or assertive, Bernstein's asymmetrical rhythms lull and lilt throughout.

This partial recital of dance genres and rhythms present or hinted at in Bernstein's concert music is designed to highlight what seems to be a central characteristic of his music, and one that has often been overlooked while discussions of his harmonic "conservatism" have gone on and on. The rhythmic life of Bernstein's music, and the dance characteristics evoked therein, are worth pointing out not only because of the frequency with which they appear, but also because they offer another handle to grasp in dealing with the question of eclecticism and "genuine" American music.

For a century, at least, American composers have been plagued by attempts to define whether or not the music any given musician has created is "American." American music is harder to pin down than, say, Hungarian or Norwegian music, because our history is so much more complex, and because new threads are constantly being woven into the fabric. With each passing decade, the blend is richer and more elaborate; composers encounter a wider background to their own experience, not something exotic to be borrowed for mere nationalistic purposes, but a range of possibilities to be used confidently because they express something about who the composer truly is.

The issue was defined by a distinguished turn-of-the-century American composer, George Chadwick. The finest praise Chadwick could bestow on his colleagues was that "they have the courage to write *themselves* down," that is, to compose music out of their own experience, to present themselves without apology for being what they were, despite the fact that it was (in Chadwick's words) "the style for dirty nosed little newspaper reviewers to speak patronizingly" of them for doing so.

Leonard Bernstein has shown, throughout a half-century of activity as a composer, that he has felt and heard and absorbed as much of the wealth of musical ideas, styles, and characteristics as anyone. He has blended them with his own concerns, both musical and extra-musical, to produce a substantial body of diverse compositions, for the concert hall and the theater, that say something very precise about what it is to be a musician and an American in the latter half of the twentieth century. Even those who dislike Bernstein's music admit that it reflects the man totally. That is the best that can be said of any artist, and no one would deny that Leonard Bernstein has had the courage to "write *himself* down."

Halil, *sketch of the opening section. Title in Hebrew at center, short score, 1981.*

4

Teacher

Of all the aspects of Leonard Bernstein's very public career, the one that is probably least known to most of his audiences is that of mentor to young musicians. He has consistently offered to the next generation the kind of support, encouragement, and inspiration that he received from his own teachers, particularly from Serge Koussevitzky at Tanglewood. At some point in almost every summer since 1940 Bernstein has returned to Tanglewood. His visits have emphasized work with the Fellows of the Tanglewood Music Center, particularly the conducting fellows, whom he coaches in the preparation of a concert in which he also takes part. "Bernstein week" is always fraught with intensity: for many of the young musicians, it remains etched in the memory as the central component of a vital period in their lives—and not simply from the fact that Leonard Bernstein was once a student in the same program and has made it big, but rather from the all-encompassing nature of his teaching.

There is no single way that Bernstein changes the lives of young conductors. Michael Tilson Thomas did not even meet him until after Thomas had won the Koussevitzky Prize at Tanglewood; shortly thereafter Thomas made a dramatic last-minute replacement for an ailing William Steinberg in a Boston Symphony Orchestra concert in New York, much as Bernstein had begun his conducting career thirty-five years earlier by substituting for Bruno Walter at the New York Philharmonic. John Mauceri had only the briefest of Tanglewood experiences with him, because in 1971 Bernstein was finishing his Mass for the opening of the Kennedy Center, but Mauceri worked with him on special projects later. Carl St. Clair had the "classical" Bernstein experience, with a full session of coaching for a memorable concert to celebrate Aaron Copland's eighty-fifth birthday and much opportunity to observe rehearsals. For all three conductors, as their essays here confirm, Bernstein played an indelible role in shaping both musicianship and a view of music in the world.

The Principle of Hope

by LEONARD BERNSTEIN

M AY I take the liberty of skipping the customary formal salu-
tations to my learned colleagues, honored guests, *et alii*, and
address myself directly to you, my young friends, who have come
here to work at Tanglewood. Thirty years ago, almost to the day, I
was sitting there, almost where you're sitting—a couple of hundred
yards from there; this building wasn't up then—but there I was
sitting, in a state of wild excitement and anticipation. It was the first
day of the first season of the Berkshire Music Center, and I had just
miraculously been accepted by its founder and director, Serge Koussevitzky, as one of his conducting students. And Koussevitzky was
standing here, so to speak, where I am today. I don't know if I can
even begin to give you an idea of what that felt like—what Koussevitzky represented then in the world of music, what radiance ema-
nated from him, what it was like to be in his presence. He was a
man possessed by music, by the ideas and ideals of music, and a man
whose possessedness came at you like cosmic rays, whether from the
podium or in a living room or in a theater like this. You see, in all
the years I had lived and grown up in Boston, I had never met
Koussevitzky: for me he was that distant glamorous figure that I saw
and heard from the dizzying height of the second balcony in Symphony Hall, and it was only after I had graduated from Harvard and
had spent a long winter studying in Philadelphia that I read in the

On July 8, 1970, the Berkshire Music Center marked its thirtieth anniversary. Leonard
Bernstein, who had recently been named along with Gunther Schuller and Seiji Ozawa as
a director of the center, delivered the welcoming address to the newly-arrived participants.
Following a tradition going back to Koussevitzky in 1940, he spoke of the arts—and
music in particular—as having an important role to play in society at large. The United
States was embroiled in an increasingly unpopular war in southeast Asia, and cynicism
spread rapidly among the nation's youth. It was in this context that Bernstein chose to
speak affirmatively of the young and of the future.

*The Tanglewood troika, 1970: Gunther Schuller, Seiji Ozawa,
Leonard Bernstein (wearing Koussevitzky's cape)*

newspaper of the impending opening of this new Music Center at Tanglewood. I rushed up to Boston armed with letters of recommendation from anybody who would give me one, gained entry into the Maestro's study, and—I must confess I was so awestruck, I don't remember a moment of that interview, except his saying at the end of it, "Of course, my dear, I vill accept you in my class." Unquote. Faint. Fade-out. Fade-in, and I'm sitting there, where you are, July 8, 1940.

And the great Koussevitzky was standing here talking to us. He was talking about commitment—commitment to art, devotion to music, dedication to one's work. I remember his using the phrase "the Central Line"—I'll never forget that—meaning the line to be followed by the artist at any cost, the line leading to perpetual discovery, a mystical line to truth as it is revealed in the musical art. It was an inspirational kind of speech—by which I mean something other than "inspiring": which it was—immensely inspiring. But besides that, it was an "inspirational" kind of speech, full of phrases that I suppose today would be smiled at as old-fashioned clichés. Does anyone speak of "dedication" any more, or "commitment"? Does one dare, in 1970, to speak of "values" or of "virtues" such as hard work, faith, mutual understanding, *patience*?

Well, the answer is *yes*; one does dare. Even though it's thirty years later, and I'm not Koussevitzky with his inspirational oratory, and you're not in any mood to listen to it. You've had a bellyful of rhetoric, I know that. So have I. But here I am, standing in this place, bearing the title of Adviser, and as the senior member of this triumvirate, I am called upon to advise you. Advice comes cheap—we all know that. It's too easy to give, and too hard to give sincerely and with clarity, precisely because today is not thirty years ago. Something basic has changed. Let's see if I can make you feel something about the difference between then and now, and then perhaps we can level with each other.

We who were sitting there in 1940 were a generation of hopers. We came out of the Roosevelt decade, the thirties, educated by the Great Depression, the National Recovery effort, which was a great social spasm in our history. We were filled with causes: we had Spain, China, Czechoslovakia, the labor movement, racial equality, antifascism. We were dedicated to social progress and to the end of fascism in all forms. We kids who had spent our college days marching with strikers, giving one benefit after another for one cause or another— we kids were committed to the future. We had hope.

Whereas now all I hear from the youth is tales of despair, hopelessness. I have spent long hours this last year sitting with university students, in America and abroad, and rapping with them—but mostly listening. And what I hear is a constant refrain of hopelessness. The system is too big, too evil. You can't fight it except by extremist action, and how many of us are extremists? You can't cope with the madness of a divided world—again, after thirty years!—a world divided into two mindless juggernauts who are even now doing battle by proxy in Southeast Asia and in the Middle East. And most of these students cannot identify with either side, so they have no cause; and the result is hopelessness. And that's the main difference between us then and you now.

Perhaps we can see this difference with more clarity in terms of music. In fact, the clarity is startling when you think about it. In the decade surrounding 1940 the key to musical expression was nobility. We still had a form called the symphony, the noble symphony. We had the Shostakovich Fifth for the first time; the Prokofiev Fifth for the first time; Copland's Third; towering symphonic works by Hindemith, Bartók, Roy Harris, Bill Schuman; and what may have been the last of them all, Stravinsky's great Symphony in Three Movements. All this music was heroic music; it spoke of struggle and triumph; it reflected the basic nobility of man. And there stood Serge Koussevitzky, ready and eager to play them all.

Now, today, all that is gone. The symphonic life that we lead—and it is a flourishing one—is no longer fed by the noble symphony, nor is it fed by much of anything else, for that matter. New music has splintered into dozens of movements, groups, and experiments, ranging from the most didactic superserialism to the most frivolous Dada. And in between these extremes some of it is fascinating, some is titillating, some of it is touching and even beautiful, and some merely opportunistic—but one thing it almost never is is *noble*. And this negativism ranges right across the arts into almost all thinking disciplines, so that these university students I see and meet with barely know where to turn. One after another they tell me, "Well, look, there's nothing to write but protest, there's nothing to sing but satire, there's nothing to feel but irony and despair. So we drown ourselves in decibels of rock, we drop out with dope; we don't know what else to do." Even the most taciturn, the bitterest, bushiest radicals I've met on campus break down after four hours of rapping and beg me to tell them what to do. "We have no leaders," they say; "we

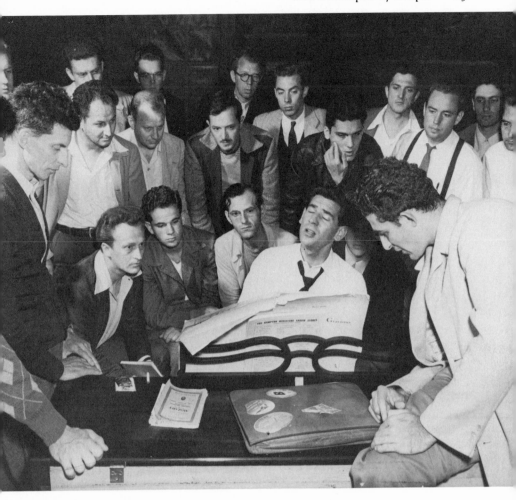

Bernstein analyzing Ravel's Alborada del Gracioso *for a Tanglewood class, summer 1948*

have no models, no idols, no heroes. The only heroes we have sometimes are in the pop field, and they change every three minutes. Or
a couple of radical leaders that not all of us can accept." One of
them said to me, "What do you expect us to feel when we have
grown up watching one hero after another being shot down before
our eyes—both Kennedys, Malcolm X, Martin Luther King?" I have
nothing brilliant to answer to that. I have nothing brilliant or immortal to say to any of you who feels despair. Of course, I can reach
back to Serge Koussevitzky and retrieve his sense of commitment,
his dedication and patience, and pass them on to you. I can do that,
and I do do that; and I wish that were enough—now, thirty years
later. But it isn't enough, we know that; something has changed. So
I have to tell you something else—maybe not brilliant or immortal,
but something very important—about the nature of despair.

I have been reading an extraordinary book, which unfortunately
exists only in German, called *Das Prinzip Hoffnung*—"The Principle
of Hope"—by the contemporary German philosopher Ernst Bloch.
That's a coincidence, that name, Ernst Bloch: this Bloch is not the
composer of *Schelomo*, but a poetic-historico-psycho-philosopher in
the great German tradition of Hegel and Nietzsche and Marx and
Freud, and he's very much at the forefront of thinking today among
the German-speaking youth. It seems really remarkable that this
Bloch, having once fled Germany during the Nazi period and now
once again having left East Germany for West Germany, should
produce as his major philosophical work a book called "The Principle
of Hope." And yet he has, and in it he demonstrates in the most
convincing way that this principle is an absolute, in the Platonic
sense, and that in a purely scientific sense hope resides in us. He
describes an aspect of consciousness that goes beyond Freud, which
he calls the "Not-Yet-Conscious"—*das Noch-Nicht-Bewusste*—
which is the psychic representation of the Not-Yet-Become: is that
too hard? The Not-Yet-Happened, *das Noch-Nicht-Gewordene*—in
other words, that which has not yet happened, but which is sensed
in anticipation. And he shows that this Not-Yet-Consciousness is just
as integral a part of man's total Consciousness as is the Unconscious
or the Subconscious of Freud, and that man does not exist without
it. This built-in Anticipation is a *quality* of man—he calls it "Dreaming Ahead," "Dreaming Forward" . . . I don't know how to translate
it: *Träumen nach Vorwärts*—and it works like a precognition, sensing what is to come; it colors and shapes our dreams, daydreams,

our wish-fulfillment drives. In other words, it's what we ordinary laymen call Hope—only a scientific description of Hope.

Now, the moment we apply this psychological force to living history, we see the trouble beginning. Because the timing of the two doesn't always work out right; you see, a crucial social change, something "Not-Yet-Become" like universal justice, racial equality, the end of war, can seem to be imminent, just within our grasp, and when it doesn't come it causes a great frustration. It may skip a generation or more, it may lie dormant for innumerable reasons, and suddenly awaken in its own time. But the youth today cannot wait: their great problem is massive impatience, sensing the changes that must come, and wanting them *now*, as a baby cries to be fed at the instant it senses hunger. And this has always been the problem of youth, the hardest obstacle of youth to overcome; in fact, all of growing up is simply the overcoming of infantile impatience. That's what we call maturity: the overcoming of impatience; and many of us never reach it—especially today.

How much harder it is to come to terms with impatience today, in an age which is so hectically speeded up, in which you take for granted instant knowing of all world events, problems, and catastrophes, and demand an equally instant remedy. It's an age in which instant gratification is offered by the advertising media—*instant* headache relief, *instant* energy, *instant* tranquilization. It's also an age in which *instant* destruction of the human race is a real possibility we all live with day and night. You grew up in this age: you are the Instant Generation. How can we expect you to be patient?

And there lies the real cause of the famous "generation gap": we grew up before all this instantaneousness and you grew up after it. And the dividing line between us is Hiroshima. To quote the great scientist Albert Szent-Gyorgyi, you've got the atom in you, we just know about it; you were born with it, we just learned about it. That's a marvelous book, by the way, Szent-Gyorgyi's new little book— have you come across it? It's called *The Crazy Ape*, and I wish you'd all read it. It's short and it's in English, unlike Bloch's book, and once you read it you will understand why Hiroshima is the crucial dividing point.

At the moment of Hiroshima the Berkshire Music Center was five years old. Today it's thirty years old. And in that intervening span of twenty-five years resides the new generation—which is you. Of course you are impatient: how could you not be impatient, growing

up in a world of instant knowing, with the promise of instant gratification, and the threat of instant overkill?

Not that we're trying to cop out, we oldies. We can't cop out. We
prepared you very carefully: we made you the best-educated generation the world has ever known, the most sophisticated, the most
politically oriented, the best read, the most informed, best equipped
for a democratic society. We saw to that. We taught you to believe,
and to expect, that the world could work; that all mouths could be
fed—every last Eskimo and Hottentot; and that no man need ever
again raise a gunsight at another; that the world is rich and blooming,
there is enough for all—enough food and clothing and music and
leisure and love. All we have to do is find the simple means of
distributing it all, fairly and universally. We taught you all that; we
taught you to hope as no one has ever hoped before in history; we
developed your sense of the "Not-Yet," your Forward-Dreaming. We
developed that to a boiling point.

But there's a catch: because what we taught you was what we
learned *before* Hiroshima. We taught you that there need never be a
war again; but what you learned from us was that there *must* never
be a war again, because then the world is finished. We talked and
you heard, but between the talking and the hearing, the linguistics
had changed. How were we to know that the dropping of a bomb
on Hiroshima would make every one of you stranger to us; that
what we had learned and would now pass on to you would auto-
matically undergo a chemical change because of the phenomenon of
instantaneousness?

So okay, you say, thanks a lot; we've learned about progress and
democracy and international brotherhood and racial equality and the
elimination of the class struggle—so okay, thanks very much, where
is it? Where are they? Let's have it! Peace, freedom, United Nations,
all this stuff you talked about—where are they? You told us there
could never be political prisoners again after the defeat of Nazism:
so what's new in Greece and Nigeria and Russia—and Chicago, for
that matter? What's a United Nations without China in it? What do
you mean, international brotherhood, when national boundaries have
never been tighter? What do you mean, peace, when the whole world
is being juggled and inflamed by two superpowers?

Well, you're right, you're absolutely right. And thank God you're
impatient, because—and this is the whole point—because that impatience is a certain signal of hope—yes, hope. You couldn't feel that

Bernstein delivering "The Principle of Hope" at the opening exercises of Tanglewood, 1970

impatience, that urge for instant dream fulfillment, if you didn't feel hope. Then what is this despair we keep hearing about? The answer is it's not despair—it's impatience, frustration, *fury*: let's go; all right, already; enough talk; enough with political self-seeking, and power grabs, and hate campaigns. Enough with guns, and blood all over our TV sets, all over our consciences. Enough with black-white-red-pinko-Commie-fascist-faggot-hippie hatreds. You're right: *enough*. But the solution is not going to come like instant gratification, like mother's milk, like televised headache relief. It's going to take a lot of doing; and you've got the overwhelming problem of relearning patience—patience, that old-fashioned word which is still as relevant as it ever was. So you see, we are back to Koussevitzky's morality after all, atom or no atom. Hiroshima generation gap or not. Because the need for instant gratification is still the mark of infancy, and the instant remedy can be just as dangerous and foolish as the instant overkill.

Nothing comes instantly except death, and every generation has to learn that anew, including yours. Nobody is going to dream on Sunday of becoming a great oboe player and wake up Monday being one, or a great composer, or a world-saving statesman. And social democracy is a hard proposition—it's harder than playing the oboe, believe me. Nobody ever said it was easy; it just *sounds* easy. Good Lord, our own country is not yet two hundred years old. There's still hope for everything; even patriotism—a word that is being defiled every day—even patriotism can be rescued from the flag-wavers and bigots. It's true that we have to work faster and harder if we're going to take our next social step before the overkill stops us dead in our tracks; but if anybody can do it, faster and harder and better, it's you, the best generation in history.

And especially you here today, *artists* of that generation. Because it's the artists of the world, the feelers and the thinkers, who will ultimately save us; who can articulate, educate, defy, insist, sing and shout the big dreams. Only the artists can turn the "Not-Yet" into reality. All right, how do you do it? Like this: Find out what you can do well, uniquely well—that's what studying is for: to find out what you can do particularly well. You. Unique. And then do it for all you're worth. And I don't mean "Doing your own thing," in the hip sense. That's passivity, that's dropping out, that's not doing anything. I'm talking about *doing*, which means—another old-fashioned phrase—serving your community, whether that community is a tiny town or six continents. And there's no time to lose, which makes your position twice as difficult, because you're caught in a paradox. You see, you've got to work fast, but not be in a hurry. You've got to be patient, but not passive. You've got to recognize the hope that exists in you, but not let impatience turn it into despair. Does that sound like double-talk? Well, it is, because the paradox exists. And out of this paradox *you* have to produce the brilliant synthesis. We'll help you as much as we can—that's why we're here— but it is you who must produce it, with your new, atomic minds, your flaming, angry hope, and your secret weapon of art. If there are still any among you who doubt that you possess hope in you, I will now prove you wrong. You surely have hopes that this speech has reached an end; well, congratulations: your hopes are fulfilled. Thank you.

Then and now: (above) *Michael Tilson Thomas conducting the orchestra of the Music Center at Tanglewood, 1970,* (below) *Thomas as conductor and soloist in* Rhapsody in Blue, *Tanglewood, July 4, 1986*

Learning from Lenny

by MICHAEL TILSON THOMAS

I MET Leonard Bernstein for the first time one day after the Tanglewood season of 1968. We played music, talked, went to the theater. It was a great day.

I next heard from him the morning after my last-minute Lincoln Center debut—he was the first to call me to congratulate me. (Amazing to think now that he was awake at eight o'clock in the morning!) After attending my first Carnegie Hall concert the next night he reaffirmed his approval of the musical path I was on and encouraged me to undertake the challenges that, as he knew better than anyone else, were awaiting me in the years ahead.

Those first East Coast years were exciting, but tough and lonely. I had to learn enormous amounts of new repertoire in a highly public atmosphere. What made that time so hard was the illness and death of my major musical mentors Ingolf Dahl, John Crown, and Gregor Piatagorsky. There I was, facing musical, social, and political crises every day, alone.

Lenny and Felicia sensed this profoundly. Lenny would invite me to attend his New York concerts or to drop by to look at his score of a piece I was working on. But it was Felicia who really made me feel at home—meeting me or, even better, making me feel free to drop by for lunch with the family and inviting me to be part of the family on holidays. I would join them in the country and be part of the warm and challenging life they shared; and inevitably during the

Californian Michael Tilson Thomas won the Koussevitzky Prize in 1968, during his first summer as a conducting fellow at Tanglewood, and was named assistant conductor of the Boston Symphony Orchestra in the spring of 1969 and associate conductor the following year. He has been music director of the Buffalo Philharmonic (1971–1979) and frequently guest conducts all over the world.

day Lenny and I would spend hours looking at the new pieces I was feverishly learning.

Lenny's patience and generosity were extraordinary. He never just told me how he did it; rather he would ask questions: "Why do you think this is written like this? What do these notes mean? How could this feeling you have for the music be best expressed or achieved? Why does Beethoven do it differently this time?"

The questions and answers, the singing and playing, flew back and forth between us, along with improvised lyrics, alternative harmonizations, tune-sleuthing, bits of poetry and literature, music history, big laughs, great sighs. We rejoined the family with the excited spirits of explorers on the trail of a great discovery bursting to share what we had learned.

Lenny has always encouraged us all to discover ourselves in the music and to sing and play it the way we feel it must be. This message continues with the example of his intellectual rigor and energy, which have been a model for several generations of us. The whole world recognizes Leonard Bernstein as a great musician. How lucky are we here at Tanglewood who know him as the steadfast and generous friend that he is.

Preparing for the Pit

by JOHN MAUCERI

By the middle of the summer of 1971, the mood among the students at Tanglewood was anything but happy. There seemed to be much dissatisfaction everywhere, and it was the first time in my life that I was aware of competition. I can still remember meeting the other conducting fellows, as well as the auditors. We did not like one another. When we got a chance to conduct, there was a general feeling that whoever was waving his arms was incompetent while the rest of us were temporarily joined together in holier-than-thou-ness. We felt that Bruno Maderna was not equipped to teach conducting; after all, he was a *composer*. And Michael Tilson Thomas was our age and very lucky. What could *he* possibly know? We were stupid and arrogant, and we wanted desperately to succeed (i.e., win the Koussevitzky Prize and become famous, just as lucky Michael had done two years before). We might never have known just how stupid and arrogant we were had Leonard Bernstein not come. But he did, and for only a week right in the middle of the summer.

"Just wait until Lenny comes," Michael would say to me with fire in his eyes. What could he mean? More of this only times ten. Times a hundred. I was suspicious.

I think I have always been suspicious of success. Perhaps I was brought up that way. Leonard Bernstein was the second conductor I had ever seen. The other was also on television, and he was Arturo

John Mauceri has conducted on Broadway, in the concert hall, and especially in the opera house, including the Metropolitan, New York City, Santa Fe, and San Francisco Opera companies. He led the European premiere of Bernstein's *Mass* in Vienna and three of the most significant productions of *Candide*, the Broadway revival and the two "opera-house" versions in New York and Glasgow. He urged the reshaping of *A Quiet Place* after its unsuccessful premiere in Houston and conducted both the American and European premieres of the revised version.

John Mauceri speaking with Leonard Bernstein at Seranak following a performance of Beethoven's Missa solemnis *at Tanglewood, 1971*

Toscanini. There was not much music in my home, but there was a television, and I practically lived inside it when I wasn't playing the piano or creating new shows for my puppet theater. Toscanini was one of those great and gray figures on the oblong screen that brought the entire world into my living room in the early 1950s. There were also Picasso, Dali, Milton Berle, Einstein, Señor Wences, Wanda Landowska, Maurice Evans, Kookla and Ollie, James Thurber, Helen Traubel, and Jimmy Durante. Sometime during all that there was Leonard Bernstein on *Omnibus*, a television series whose name was a great mystery to me. I watched a number of these programs and later watched a number of his *Young People's Concerts* on television. I wasn't sure I liked Leonard Bernstein, but I had to keep watching.

And then there was *West Side Story* when I was thirteen and really knew everything there was to know about Broadway. I could, after all, recite whole scenes from *Oklahoma!* and *South Pacific* from memory. I had staged *The King and I* in my back yard when I was ten. Because my older brother was feature editor of our high school newspaper (yes, I'll admit it: it was called *The Jet Gazette*), I got to be the drama critic at age fourteen. I remember seeing *West Side Story* with my brother at a matinée. I had just seen *The Music Man*, which I loved, and *West Side Story* did not seem as good to me. I remember finding the musical a bit pretentious and its staging somewhat repetitive: side wagons and then a central area for the big scenes, and then side wagons. Added to this, the oboist cracked on his big solo, and that ruined everything.

So now Leonard Bernstein was coming to Tanglewood. "Just wait," Michael said again.

We conductors were required to sing in the Festival Chorus, and Bernstein would conduct only one work that summer: Beethoven's *Missa solemnis*. Bernstein was completing his first major composition in years: *Mass*, for the opening of the Kennedy Center. Because of that he could only come to Tanglewood for a week. We would attend his BSO rehearsals and sing in the chorus, and he would see us conduct with the student orchestra and tell us what he thought. And that would be that.

OVERLEAF: *Beethoven's* Missa solemnis *at Tanglewood on July 25, 1971; soloists (left to right) are bass Sherrill Milnes, tenor Walter Cochran, alto Maureen Forrester, and soprano Phyllis Curtin*

The first rehearsal was for the chorus alone on the stage of the Shed. It was in the evening, and we were all tired and even grumpier than usual, but there was Leonard Bernstein—Lenny—himself. And we began to rehearse "this other guy's Mass," as Lenny called it. After three hours we had gotten nowhere. More than half the work remained unrehearsed because we had spent so much time on the opening pages. When the Maestro was told we had to stop, he looked at us in surprise. Now what? The orchestra rehearsal was the next morning at ten. "Well, we could stay," said one of us. "Or we could all show up at seven tomorrow morning," another one of us suggested. I was ready to do both.

I don't remember if we did either. I only remember going back to the dorm and walking around outside and crying. In three hours he had reminded us of who we were and what we had to do to be worthy of calling ourselves musicians. Lenny had come to Tanglewood, and I now understood that look in Michael's eyes.

*   *   *

The day soon came for us to conduct in front of Leonard Bernstein. In order to prepare, my colleagues had disappeared during lunch. For some reason I felt secure enough not to study Tchaikovksy's *Romeo and Juliet* one more time but rather to stay on the grounds, and this decision meant lunch with Bernstein. The first bit of technical advice I received was the last thing I expected to hear. The Maestro wanted to know the tempo relationship between the slow introduction and the Allegro that followed. I learned his theory that the great masterworks have basically one tempo from beginning to end and that the different speeds within that masterwork are all mathematically related. I somehow expected a lesson in "feeling" the music. That, of course, came later—after the temporal structures had been delineated in my mind. (Surely this is the basis of my theory of temporal structures as the basic compositional element in Verdi's operas, a theory I recently explained to Lenny, much to his delight and interest.)

In those days I wore a Mickey Mouse watch, with a bright red band. I vividly remember preparing the orchestra for the first notes of *Romeo and Juliet* and hearing Lenny, who was standing in the percussion section, say, "I wonder what Tchaikovsky would say, seeing you with that watch on your wrist, about to conduct *Romeo and Juliet!*" Everyone had a good laugh, and then for the next twenty minutes I was on.

The next day in a small room he told each of us what he thought. I remember he thought Charles Darin the most talented and Tom Michalek the most professional. My beat was "expressive but repetitive." Then came the performance of the *Missa solemnis* and then he was gone.

* * *

It took me almost a year to find him again, because I had only just begun to learn that he was gone. A member of the Yale Symphony (of which I was music director) was playing in the revival of *Mass* that was rehearsing in New York before re-opening in Washington. I attended rehearsals and volunteered to assist conductor Maurice Peress, an offer that was gladly accepted. In Washington, just at the moment I was giving up hope of ever seeing Bernstein again, and on the day of the one-and-only preview at the Kennedy Center, he arrived and busily greeted everyone. I thought he would never remember me, but when we bumped into each other backstage, he did, and I uttered the fateful words I never planned to say: "Mr. Bernstein, do you need someone to take notes for you this evening during the preview?" "What a good idea! Harry, give John a ticket to sit next to me in the box tonight."

I called my wife Betty in New Haven. Assistant for the night! What if I coughed? How does one write notes in the dark? Get a small flashlight, a big pad of paper, and a black marker pen. And don't screw up. . . .

The lights came down at the Kennedy Center Opera House. In the dark the composer entered the center box. "Cover the red light on the lamp in the pit," was his first note to me. "More shotgun on Allen" was another. "Less Roxychord here." And so it went: notes on lighting, amplification, tempo, and diction, in a language I only partially understood. Needless to say he did not miss a thing. The next day I took notes during the last rehearsal by sitting behind Maurice to get his comments while holding a walkie-talkie in my hand to receive messages from Bernstein, many rows back! Only later did I learn what it was like to conduct Bernstein's music with him present. Maurice was a good sport, and to this day I remember this absurd scene whenever I am in the pit and Lenny, a number of rows

behind, is giving notes to some budding Maestrino who fully expects
to do much better than I am doing at that moment.

It was late that summer that Lenny asked me to be his assistant
for a new production of *Carmen* at the Met. Goeren Gentele, the
newly appointed general manager of the Met and the producer of
this new *Carmen*, had been killed in an automobile accident, and
Lenny wanted his own musical assistant to help out. When the
telephone rang in my New Haven apartment, I was working on my
dissertation ("The Structural Uses of Orchestration in Early Twentieth-Century Music") and my adviser had told me the day before
that he wasn't sure it was really going to be a successful subject.
Harry Kraut called and said Lenny needed an assistant for *Carmen*.
He would pay me one thousand dollars. "I would pay *you* one
thousand dollars," I thought, but I said, "When do you want me to
start?" "Tomorrow," was the answer. "Wait a moment, I'll put Lenny
on." Click, click. "Giovanni? Are you going to do it?" I thought
about my dissertation for a millisecond. "Yes, of course." And in the
next moment LB had accidentally cut me off. He was gone. I called
Betty at work: "Silliman College Master's Office." "Leonard-
BernsteinjustcalledmeandwantsmetobehisassistantIstarttomorrow-
Bye," I said, in time to hear the phone ring for the return call from
LB and loud enough for the master in the next office to shout to
Betty, "What great news!" The next minute I was getting directions
to Leonard Bernstein's house in Connecticut. I was expected in the
morning.

The next month became the basis of my professional life. I attended
every meeting, rehearsal, and performance; discussed tempos, costumes, methods of achieving one's artistic goals; watched the master's
ability to compromise when called for and to reject compromise when
that was called for. I was about to be twenty-seven, and Lenny was
about to be fifty-four. I was half his age—something I would never
be again—and after ten years of going to the old and new Mets, I
was standing *behind* the gold curtain.

When I returned to Yale that fall, I attended the master's tea at
Silliman College. When asked about my summer, I said excitedly that
I had become Leonard Bernstein's assistant on *Carmen* at the Met.
The look I received was one I'd never seen aimed at me before. What
was implied I had never experienced before. What was not said was
terrible.

For a moment, that day, I wanted to reassure everyone that I was still me—the same John, wearing his Mickey Mouse watch. I was just having the opportunity of a lifetime, learning from the greatest musical teacher in the world. But in a moment I realized that nothing I could say would change the minds that had now been made up and had closed tight. I saw myself on the other side of the looking glass, and these former friends and colleagues had their noses pressed against the glass. For them I would never be the same. And now that I think of it, I suppose they were right.

Mauceri and Bernstein in Glasgow during rehearsals for the "expanded opera-house version" of Candide, *May 1988*

Bernstein gives advice to Carl St. Clair as he prepares a performance of Copland's Clarinet Concerto, 1985.

Coaching for Copland

by CARL ST. CLAIR

I GREW up in Texas playing the trumpet in school bands. Not until I was in college did I learn what a great orchestra could sound like, and when I did, it was Leonard Bernstein who showed me. While waiting for a friend to pick me up for a party, I turned on the television to pass the time until he arrived. By sheer accident, I happened on a concert of Leonard Bernstein conducting the Boston Symphony Orchestra in Tchaikovsky's Fifth Symphony at Tanglewood. At that time I knew Bernstein only as the composer of *West Side Story*. I'd never heard any music of Tchaikovsky, I'd never heard of Tanglewood, and I'd never heard of Koussevitzky. All the newness that was going on in this black-and-white Westinghouse TV was so overwhelming that I couldn't go to the party.

In the summer of 1985, when I was a conducting fellow at Tanglewood, I knew that they were going to select some of us to appear on an all-Copland concert with Bernstein. I wondered whether I should let somebody know how much it meant to me, because of the experience I've just described, to be one of those chosen people. But one night, studying in my room, I decided, No, that's futile, and it's also not trusting. If it doesn't happen, it is an omen, and if it does happen, that's also an important sign. I'd learned to listen to these voices and to try to follow and trust, rather than try to create opportunities. And in the end I was told, "We'd like you to do the Clarinet Concerto."

I got my first impression of Bernstein at Seranak, where our conducting classes were held. Of course, everyone was there early, waiting in anticipation. Many of us, including me, had never seen him in

---

Texas-born Carl St. Clair taught at the University of Michigan School of Music before being named assistant conductor of the Boston Symphony Orchestra in 1986.

person, so we didn't know what to expect. When he walked into the room—Koussevitzky's living room, with a wonderful full-length portrait of Koussevitzky at the end—he struck me first as not nearly as tall as I had imagined, but with a great deal of presence.

The first thing he did was take in two or three big breaths. He said, "It always takes me a minute or two to put myself into this room and get my mind to realizing where I am and how much this room has meant to me." He looked around at the pictures, and he greeted the two pianists, who have been at Tanglewood for a long time. When he comes into a room, he does lots of hugging and embracing and touching. He takes energy from everybody he touches. He needs that energy from people, but he gives it back with his love and inspiration. Whatever he takes from you, you get back with interest. And that's why I always felt that I needed to be as open as I could while I was around him, so that I could get as much as I could from him.

Then he asked, "Where are my six guys?" meaning the six conducting fellows that summer. We were individually introduced to him, and the three of us conducting in the Copland concert were identified. Then we sat down to begin the class.

We worked on several pieces, but the two that were most memorable for me were the Beethoven Second Symphony and the Brahms Fourth Symphony. We spent about two and a half hours on the first nine bars or less of Beethoven's Second Symphony, first movement. I had conducted the piece before; I had studied it a lot. It was on the summer repertoire list that we were supposed to learn, so I'd restudied it. Yet after two hours of looking at that passage with his vision, through his eyes as conductor, composer, writer, man of the world, musician, pianist—I realized that I hadn't really seen anything ever before in those notes.

He talked about the way a particular note leads to the next; about the voicing of some chords; about the reminiscence of a certain downward flute scale which comes in the Ninth Symphony—and then he'd go to the piano and play part of the Ninth Symphony. It got more and more involved as he proceeded. "And he uses this same thing in another symphony,"—so he'd play and sing that—"and you *do* recall this string quartet, which was written at the same time." It just got deeper and deeper. And all this information is at the tips of his fingers. Just looking at those notes through his eyes made me realize another world of perceiving and understanding music.

Bernstein coaching Tanglewood conducting fellows (above)
Grant Llewellyn and (below) *James Ross in the living room of*
Koussevitzky's home, Seranak, 1985.

I was also knocked out by the fact that he was speaking at least five languages in that room, because we had people from all over the world. So he spoke in Dutch, and Italian, and French, and German, and English, and a few words in Japanese . . . just carrying on conversations. It boggled me, completely and totally.

Those days at Seranak were phenomenal for everybody. We'd go out feeling, on the one hand, totally renewed because of what we'd learned and because of the inspiration and energy that we got from him, and, on the other hand, totally useless from realizing all those things we'd studied but never seen before! Yet he pointed them out to us with love; it was never, "You *should* have looked at it," but rather, "Let's discover it!" and "Why?"

He never forces anyone to conduct the way he conducts. He never demonstrated much for us, because he didn't want us to copy him. He never insists that your hand be positioned a certain way, or that you use specifically the left or right, or that you follow any textbook prescriptions of how to stand and how to hold your mouth and feet and chest and eyes—none of that. For him, it all comes from the music. Yet the technique is pedagogically sound, because he's trying to allow people to discover themselves and let the music come through them, rather than superimpose something from the outside. That approach really helped us, because it deepened our own understanding of ourselves, a change that doesn't happen often if the teacher requires you to do things a certain way.

So from the technical aspect of conducting, he was very permissive. Still, he wanted to know the musical reasons for everything: why one conductor took a *rubato*, why another decided to make a *ritardando*, why another decided to hold a certain note longer or shorter, or why a given quarter note had not received its full value. If we had a reason that we had thought out, and if we conducted the passage in a convincing way, he would believe us. If we didn't know why we were doing things that way, we were in trouble! His own conducting scores show that he has thought out every note carefully: its length, its direction, where it's going, where it came from, how it touches the next note.

Of course, often, when someone stood up to conduct in that class, he or she was inhibited and very nervous because, after all, it was Leonard Bernstein in front of us. Yet within three minutes that fear would be gone. He has a way of relieving the tension without removing his presence, so that his energy and his inspiration help you.

That's a gift! Within a half-hour or forty-five minutes, people were transformed. I remember that some participants who had tried to conduct Brahms in a stiff way were suddenly moving flexibly, communicating the music more fluently than even *they* realized they could. I was the same.

Our seminars at Seranak went on and on and on—three and a half, four hours without a break. There was no end to Bernstein's energy, no end to his desire to help us, because he realized he wasn't going to be there very long. And of course that room, and the seminar, and Seranak itself all have such a deep meaning for him that he wanted to touch everybody.

And he was interested in our knowing more than music. He chastised the conducting fellows having lunch with him one day because we didn't know enough poetry. He quizzed us: "Do you read poetry?" He decreed that we didn't know enough, and then began quoting from memory—not just one or two lines of your favorite James Joyce or whomever, but long sections by American poets whose names I frankly wasn't very familiar with.

Before he arrived at Tanglewood, we had had a chance to run through our Copland pieces with the TMC orchestra, to get past the level of sight-reading. Gisela Buka was leading the *Outdoor Overture*, Hans Rottman *Inscape*; I'd started rehearsing the Clarinet Concerto, with BSO clarinettist Peter Hadcock as soloist. The concert was to be on a Wednesday; we started our rehearsals with Bernstein on Sunday night.

He was doing Copland's Third Symphony, and he took the first rehearsal, on Sunday night, all by himself for that piece. For the rest of the program, he had selected works from various periods of Copland's life to give us a good survey of his music. He loved the composer and the music so much that everything had to be just right. He kept saying, "You know, Aaron's going to be here!" You could see that he was eager for each of us to put our best foot forward.

His comments during the rehearsals for the Third Symphony were fascinating; he was determined not simply to rehearse the piece and get it to performance level, but to help the orchestra and every conductor there to learn the piece by taking it apart and showing us how it was composed: how a certain xylophone and snare drum passage is like the Shostakovich Fifth Symphony, and how that sort of expressive quality happened to Copland in his Third. The fact that we were allies with Russia at the time of its composition explained why so much of the symphony, in the voicings and the chordal structure, sounds a little like Shostakovich or Prokofiev. He took it apart, pointed out double fugues and canons, and so on. All the rehearsals went like that, because he wanted to bring this great piece to everybody in such a way that we would understand its greatness and perpetuate it in future performances. He never gave the sense of saying, "*I* know this, but I don't have time to tell you about it." He just took the time! When he is working towards a musical goal, time is not important.

I remember he worked with Gisela Buka on the introduction to the *Outdoor Overture*, where a little lilt takes place in the passage before the Allegro starts. He just *had* to get Gisela to feel it, because that lilt was Copland. It has a certain "walking" feeling, and he spent quite a bit of time just on that passage. With Hans Rottman, he was always trying to get the dramatic power of *Inscape*; it's one of Copland's latest pieces, twelve-tone and quite dramatic—and almost never done. Hans was a wonderful young guy, but Bernstein found him a little too gentle, so he tried to get him to make some of these very big blocks of sound stronger. And once Hans realized that he could work that way with this music, he did so.

With the Clarinet Concerto, he was always talking to me about inner beats in the fast movement: "Inner beat! Middle of the beat!" The style is basically jazz—not just "One–two," but "a-one-and-two-and. . . ." He was always talking about feeling that jazzy inner beat. Conducting that movement of Copland's concerto like Mozart just doesn't work. The rhythm has to have energy. And the string players, who are traditionally brought up with a legato style that is used for Mozart or Haydn string quartets, needed to learn to use the inner beat, to swing a little, in order to play what is basically a jazz style, though it also has very difficult notes and difficult rhythms.

Yet Bernstein doesn't teach simply with words. If you look at the photographs of him teaching, you can see that he is *there* completely; his total energy is with you. When he uses words, even the rhythm and the intonation of his voice demonstrate musically what he's asking for. And at the same time his body assumes a posture and his face takes a position with his eyes and hands, to give a visual demonstration. One of the great things about him as a teacher is that the meaning of the words is thus reinforced in two or three ways—to say nothing of the energy with which they are said, and the love that

All-Copland concert given by the Tanglewood Music Center
Orchestra on July 24, 1985: (top) Bernstein conducts the Third
Symphony; (bottom) he joins with the other participants to
acknowledge the applause of the audience in the Tanglewood
Shed. Left to right, Carl St. Clair, Hans Rottman, clarinettist
Peter Hadcock, Bernstein, Aaron Copland, Gisela Buka.

comes across in the words themselves. "Carl," he'd say, "we need those *inner beats*, man. . . ."

The very opening of the work is like going into a dream. And that's the section Bernstein worked on almost more than anything, to get the right feeling and tempo. I listened to two different recordings of Copland conducting it; in both cases he took it slower than his own metronome marking indicates. So I do it a little slower too; it doesn't hurt.

I was certainly nervous; it's not an easy piece to conduct, and Peter Hadcock and I didn't have very much advance notice. The organizers wanted to select the perfect program, because of the importance of the whole event as a special concert for the eighty-fifth birthday of the man who had been the head of the composition faculty at Tanglewood for twenty-five years; so they thought about it for a long time before deciding. I think we only had nine or ten days to learn the piece once the program was set.

The night of the performance, right up to the time we went on, Bernstein was backstage. He met with all of us. "How are you feeling? Doing okay?" At one point he said, "Are you nervous?" and I said, "I'm really nervous . . ." and he said, "You'd damn well better be, because this is important. If you weren't nervous, I'd kick you in the rear end!" All the time, backstage, he gave us incentive by demonstrating certain passages. He would say, "Now Gisela, don't forget . . ." and he'd sing the lilting theme. And to me he described the opening of the Clarinet Concerto, "It's like one of those *Gymnopédies*, it has that . . ." and his arm would swoop in a grand, slow gesture. He got us all into the right mood just before we went out— not so as to make us nervous but with a warm, encouraging feeling, like a coach: "Come on, team, we're doing this tonight, and we've got to pull this off for Aaron, and he's there."

Just before I walked out on stage, he put both hands on my shoulders and looked straight into my eyes, and he said, "You realize that you are going to walk on stage and conduct what I think is some of the most beautiful music ever written by a human being— and that that person is going to be sitting in the audience!" He was talking about the first movement of the Clarinet Concerto—and he's right! It's so simple and so beautiful. Whenever I've done the piece since, those memories come back: ". . . and that human being is sitting in the audience."

I'll never forget the curtain calls at the concert, and how wonderful it felt going backstage and coming forward again—especially the final time, when Copland got up on the podium. I'd never been in front of an audience that reacted with so much excitement and love, and I realized that this was a historic moment.

When I went back to Michigan after that summer, I took with me the memory of wonderful experiences—working on Beethoven's *Egmont* overture with Seiji Ozawa and the Brahms Fourth with Kurt Masur. I learned a lot about Debussy's *Prelude to the Afternoon of a Faun* from André Previn, and I learned much from Joseph Silverstein's master class. I could go on and on describing the things that touched me. But it is still the Copland week that I remember in capital letters, not only for the musical value, but for the historical value as well. When you come into the presence of a man like Copland and conduct his music and have him there at his age—especially at Tanglewood on such a special birthday—so many spirits are raised that even if there had been no music at all, it would have been a great moment. I'm still feeding off the fuel ignited that summer. I hope the seed that was planted then will grow a long, long time.

Last page of a fair copy of the Serenade *with the solo violin part and piano reduction*

5

Recording Artist

A complete discography of Leonard Bernstein's recordings as conductor would fill a good-sized book. Working with many orchestras all over the world, he has built a recorded repertory that is particularly strong in the symphonic tradition of the great Austrian and German masters from Haydn to Mahler, in the works of Igor Stravinsky, and in a whole school of contemporary American symphonists, as well as operatic recordings of powerful dramatic thrust. His New York Philharmonic recordings have played a role in the rediscoveries of Charles Ives and Carl Nielsen and have documented such modern masters as Copland, Schuman, and Harris. And even this sizable body of work by no means exhausts the range of Bernstein's recorded output, since it fails to mention Sibelius, Shostakovich, Debussy, Bartók, and many others.

The making of records is an exacting, intense business, not just for the performers—who aim at the elusive goal of a reading that is note-perfect and yet filled with the energy and life of a live performance—but also for the producer—who must keep the recording session on track, hear potential problems in the take and call them to the conductor's attention, and decide when a passage, or a complete piece, has been successfully caught "in the can."

John McClure, who produced most of Bernstein's New York Philharmonic recordings over nearly two decades, describes what it was like.

For the Record:
Leonard Bernstein in the Studio

by JOHN McCLURE

OVER the past thirty years Leonard Bernstein and I have collaborated on nearly two hundred phonograph recordings. Moreover, we are both still intact and still friends, a testament to our stamina, his blazing talent, and my natural luck. These are years I wouldn't trade for any known human benison, and ours is a professional association anyone in our industry would kill for.

That said, however, it must be acknowledged that working with Lenny, especially under the hundred-dollars-a-minute tension of American symphonic recording sessions, is only for the stress-tolerant. Lenny is demanding (how not?) and unpredictable. Not in the sense of being *whimsical*, but in the sense of his talent's making his vision unknowable. I have long since given up trying to outguess him, beyond marking a ragged ensemble or the obvious "clam," because, quite simply, I rarely know what internal musical image he has in his sights.

Over the years I have entertained in the control room a parade of exceptional musicians, many of them conductors, who have been appointed as Lenny's ears-for-the-day, and none of them have ever had any better luck than I in predicting what Lenny would like or hate about what he had just recorded. What worked last week didn't this week; what worked in Strauss didn't in Debussy; what was glorious in the first movement was execrable in the third, and so on.

John McClure started at Columbia Records in 1952 as a tape editor and became in 1957 a record producer in the Masterworks Department responsible for the final recordings of Bruno Walter and Igor Stravinsky. As music director and then director, he made records with all of the artists on Columbia's roster until he left CBS to become an independent producer of records and television audio ranging from pop to classical.

And this principle has applied not only to recording technique, but to orchestral playing as well. He has always been so far ahead of us—so deep inside the music—that we have had to scrabble continually to keep up.

The same situation applies equally to his writing, of both TV scripts and books. Proffered words or phrases are acknowledged but never used. Every sentence boils up from the rich Bernsteinian substrate, unpolluted.

This *sui generis* syndrome is highlighted by a hint of what might be clinically described as contrariness. If you praise a take, he will find flaws; if you knock it, he will defend it, thereby keeping you a bit off balance. The man is not long on patience and not stingy with blame.

Why, you ask, if this is such a high-cholesterol, low-serenity diet, do the three or four of us who have produced his work over the years keep coming back for more? It's quite simple. Beyond the exhilaration of great, imaginative music-making, any contact with the five or six talented people who walk about masquerading as Leonard Bernstein is unfailingly stimulating, educational, maddening, and musically nutritious.

I remember the first sessions we had together. From the advent of stereo in 1957 up to the moment he suddenly left CBS for television in 1959, Columbia's Masterworks Department director, David Oppenheim, had produced all Bernstein recordings. Suddenly I became music director with an instant family of artists like Stravinsky, the Mormon Tabernacle Choir, Bruno Walter, and Leonard Bernstein. Panic! Bernstein and the New York Philharmonic were on tour in Russia, and plans had been made to record Copland's *Billy the Kid* and the Shostakovich Fifth on their homecoming, which happened to be in Boston. Having cut my baby teeth two years earlier on Bruno Walter and the Columbia Symphony Orchestra in Hollywood, I was faced with three unknowns: Symphony Hall, Leonard Bernstein, and the New York Philharmonic. The latter two were ablaze from a triumphant tour, and somehow we matched them with our microphone placement, because the records became classics, and Lenny and I began our twenty years of recording partnership.

For a time we recorded in the Grand Ballroom of the St. George Hotel in Brooklyn, but when that hotel closed its doors we found a place closer to home: Manhattan Center, built early in the century by Oscar Hammerstein to house his Manhattan Opera Company.

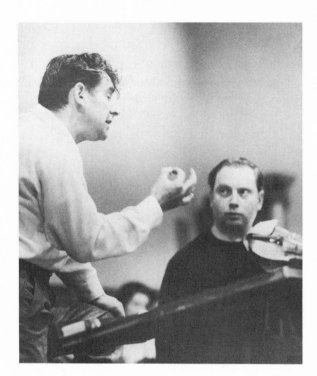

(Top) *Bernstein and Isaac Stern recording the* Serenade, *April 19, 1956.* (Bottom) *Bernstein as conductor and soloist recording the Ravel Concerto in G in London, his first recording made outside the United States, July 1, 1946.*

The building had fallen on awkward times and was used most visibly for union meetings. The Grand Ballroom was a bizarre MGM/Egyptian/art deco extravaganza, beckoning to the Radamès in us but also, in the dead of winter when the humidity was down, providing a remarkable live acoustic for many of our most vivid and exciting records.

At certain other times, this Janus-faced hall would turn on us and wrap us in a gymnasium acoustic, forcing our mikes closer, making ensemble difficult, and making Lenny sweat for every bar. But even when conditions were ideal, Lenny was not easy to please. Occasionally (once or twice each decade, as I recall), he would be delighted with what came out of the loudspeakers on the first take. But normally he would smell disaster, and we would have to perform technical and emotional trapeze acts, and even the odd con game, to get things back on track.

The worst would be those happily rare occasions when he would decide to help us balance the microphones by staying in the control room and delegating one of his assistants to conduct. This, as we would tearfully remind him, was a waste of time, since the orchestra, who had come to play for Lenny, was damned if they would put out for anyone else, no matter how disarming. We would get more and more hysterical and Lenny more frustrated, until I would literally push him out the door onto the podium so that everyone involved could get back to doing what they did best.

And his best was a miracle indeed. I certainly wasn't conscious that we were making history. We were having too much fun. American conductor, American orchestra—and complete symphonic cycles were knocked off one after the other: Brahms, Mahler, Beethoven, Tchaikovsky, Sibelius, Schumann. Then the pioneering records of Copland, Ives, Nielsen. And what we called our "junk" sessions, where we rehearsed and recorded at sight, the Strauss, Bizet, von Suppé, Thomas, Waldteufel, and Rossini mini-masterpieces that Lenny felt he couldn't program in the regular season. These were the most fun of all.

Our recording sessions were tense, joyful, suicidal, efficient, and frustrating, just like life itself, but life speeded up and condensed. They were certainly never dull, just as the man is never dull. He knows more and feels more than anyone I have ever known. The depth and accessibility of his knowledge is staggering. What the public doesn't see are the hours of lonely and painstaking preparation—the phrasing, bowing, dynamics that go into every performance. This aspect is easily overshadowed by the vivid public persona.

During the past decade, Lenny has given up recording sessions in favor of live concert recordings. It may be more efficient, but it's definitely less fun. I hope he misses those days. I know I do.

Aaron Copland, Bernstein, and John McClure listening to playbacks at a recording session in January 1964

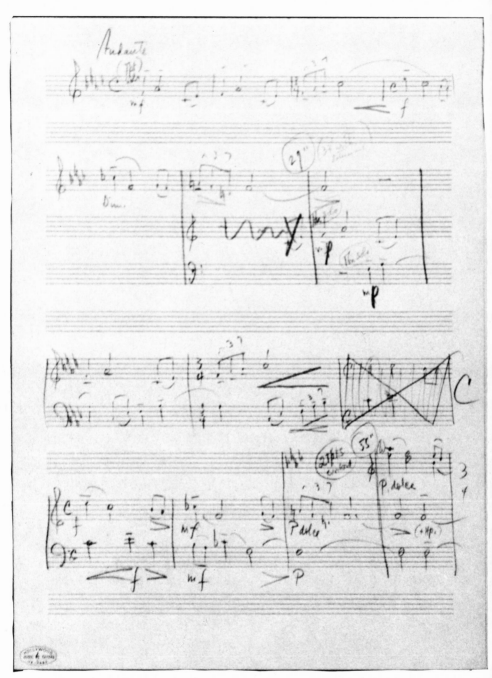

Short score sketch for the opening sequence of the film On the Waterfront, *1954*

6

Television Performer

Bernstein would have been famous without television, but his name never would have become the household word that it is even among people who have never been to an orchestra concert, without that ubiquitous staring eye that entered the American living room during the 1950s, just about the time that Bernstein began discussing Beethoven, or jazz, or Bach, or the American musical theater on CBS's Omnibus. When the new medium brought Bernstein into homes across the country, there was little serious consideration of music anywhere on the airwaves. It is at least arguable that no similar discussion of music since has matched the inventiveness, imagination, and passion of those memorable Omnibus programs of the 1950s.

The lecture-demonstrations for adults on Omnibus led to a similar inventive—and enormously influential—series of Young People's Concerts with the New York Philharmonic. Recent years have seen the development of broadcast concerts in plenty, not only from Bernstein, but from other musical entities all over the world—an enduring legacy of that early work. And the people who have been influenced by those programs in great and small ways number in the millions.

Congruent Odysseys:
Bernstein and the Art of Television

by ROBERT S. CLARK

S OME of the gifted among us are twice blessed: they yoke arresting talents to historic coincidences that enable them to make the most of their gifts. Leonard Bernstein is one of these: it was his—and our—good fortune that he and American television grew to maturity together.

I certainly don't mean to imply that, had television not existed, Bernstein's would have been anything less than the most remarkable career ever for a classically trained American musician. By the time he wrote and appeared in his first *Omnibus* telecast (November 14, 1954), the young dynamo from Lawrence, Massachusetts, had already made a lasting dent in the nation's musical consciousness, beginning with his selection as assistant conductor of the New York Philharmonic in 1943 and his subsequent and widely cheered debut appearance as a substitute for Bruno Walter on November 14 of that year; and continuing through the New York premieres of his ballet *Fancy Free* and musical comedy *On the Town* (both 1944), and the first performances of his *Jeremiah* Symphony (1944) and *Age of Anxiety* Symphony (1949). Before *Omnibus*, he had already conducted the Boston and Chicago orchestras, the London Philharmonic, the Israel Philharmonic, and the Czech Philharmonic. He had been named head of the orchestra and conducting departments of the Berkshire Music Center at Tanglewood, Massachusetts, and he had been the first American ever to conduct at La Scala, Milan, leading Maria Callas and the opera house forces in Cherubini's *Medea*.

Robert S. Clark, former editorial director of the *High Fidelity* group of magazines, is the music critic of the quarterly *Hudson Review* and a contributor to *Musical America*.

Curtain call for Cherubini's Medea *at La Scala, after Bernstein became the first American to conduct an opera there, December 10, 1953. Left to right, G. Oldani (General Secretary of La Scala), Maria Callas, Margherita Wallman (director of the production), Bernstein.*

Clearly Bernstein the musician needed no boost from the fledgling medium of television.

Yet it seems to me unarguable that the creative and re-creative career we associate today with Leonard Bernstein is indivisible from its televised manifestations. Born in 1918, only a few years before the technology's first practical devices were demonstrated, Bernstein found in the fluid and venturesome nature of the postwar medium a perfect match for one side of his burgeoning creative personality.

Bernstein's contributions to television's archives belong to three interwoven but distinct genres. First in importance, I think, are those programs in which he acts as a pedagogue and exegete for music of many different kinds—mainstream classical, contemporary classical, jazz, musical comedy, rock—and for its forms, expressive intentions, technical means, and specific character. From 1954 forward he took this role in a continuing string of appearances on *Omnibus*, *Lincoln Presents*, and *Ford Presents*, and ultimately, from 1958 until 1972, in the fifty-three programs that constitute the acclaimed *Young People's Concerts*.

A second avenue for his activity has been as composer of musical works that have been televised: his symphonies, his stage works— *Mass*, *Trouble in Tahiti*, *Wonderful Town*—and his *Chichester Psalms* are a few examples. And finally there are the numerous television films of his conducting appearances leading the New York Philharmonic, the Israel Philharmonic, and other orchestras in the works of other composers.

The first of these three contributions is indisputably both unique and important. The second is probably unique—is there another composer who can boast that so large a portion of his major works has been videotaped in performance?—but it does not impress me as especially important. The third role is an important one, but it is not unique: many conductors have had their orchestral performances transcribed by the video camera.

Although his conducting career was going great guns by the time he made his television debut—he was barely two years away from being named co-director of the New York Philharmonic—it was the pedagogical and explicative Bernstein that television exploited first. The vehicle was *Omnibus*, that thinking man's smorgasbord that graced the medium's early commercial days; broadcast concerts were still in the future.

The series got off to a slam-bang start late in 1954 with the

*Bernstein standing on the enlarged first page of Beethoven's
Fifth Symphony, broadcasting the first of his* Omnibus *programs,
November 14, 1954*

sequence devoted to Beethoven's musical sketchbooks. On and around what was probably the best prop Bernstein ever used—the studio floor transformed into a giant facsimile of musical staves—he deployed instrumentalists as stand-ins for notation and alternated these visual representations of Beethoven's first-, second-, and sometimes later-generation thoughts about now familiar passages with illustrations of the passages' sound. It was both illuminating and amusing, the musicians—unaccustomed to the glare of the camera's eye—sometimes looking like embarrassed children caught at a foolish game, and the Maestro already displaying his gift for combining homely metaphor (the "last lap" of a symphonic movement) with nutshell lessons ("The artist will give away his life and energies to be sure that one note follows another with complete inevitability"). This sequence sets an intellectual tone for practically all that is to come.

Although it was not long afterward that *Omnibus* host Alistair Cooke was hailing Bernstein, in hyperbole that hardly squares with our preconceptions of the British, as "the most articulate composer and performer around," from the perspective of the eighties the chief actor in the earliest sequences is something of a stranger. He could be a bashful young Ivy-League don, gaze averted or sinking to the floor when the camera proves too relentless, unable to erase a trace of condescension from his tone and manner. When not clutching a saving cigarette, his hands constantly seek a haven: folded over his abdomen, thrust into a side pocket or a lapel of his coat, fingertips coming together as if to form a shield. Even his movements around the sound stage resemble the striding and perching of a self-conscious professor in front of a class.

But it doesn't take Bernstein long to leave the classroom behind. By early 1957 he is less ill at ease: he has adopted a tux as standard apparel, and when a lock of hair falls rakishly across his forehead, he feels no compulsion to brush it back. He is more rhetorical and less professorial; the master of ceremonies that is to persist into the days of the *Young People's Concerts* has fully emerged. His voice has become one of his prime assets: firm, direct, never patronizing or hectoring, folksy enough to win your confidence but with a dash of elevated tone to command your attention.

In these programs, broadcast in late 1956 and early 1957, we encounter the pedagogical style that will carry over into the *Young People's Concerts*. It is a style designed to confront the middlebrow

Robert Saudek, producer of the Omnibus series, talking with Bernstein on his own level, without stooping, and to escort him gently, along the path of least resistance, to increased understanding. Bernstein most often proceeds by stating at the outset the entrenched misconceptions or unfounded assumptions of his putative audience, grownups and youngsters alike, and going on to refute them, using cozy metaphors and analogies along with musical examples and technical explanations carefully gauged not to overtax. His intention, implicit or explicit, is always to enable the music to make an emotional impact upon the newly awakened hearer.

Take his program of March 31, 1957, in which he sets out to demolish the notion—one he must assume is widely held by his audience—that the music of Johann Sebastian Bach is boring. He plunges right in by declaring that when he was a young piano student he was taken by the "immediacy" of the slow movement of Bach's Italian Concerto—and he illustrates at the piano. But, he concedes, so much of Bach can come across as endless strings of sixteenth notes chugging along unvaryingly, "more motion than emotion." Asserting that audiences today are habituated to music of dramatic contrast, he characterizes Bach's music as being "about one thing at a time." "Just as the architecture of a bridge grows inevitably out of one initial arch," Bach's musical structures are formed about a single theme or idea, and the rest is elaboration, discussion, reiteration, argumentation. "That frightening bugaboo counterpoint," he says soothingly, "is nothing to be afraid of," and he illustrates from the scores, showing at one point how the contrapuntal strands of Bach's chorale preludes resemble "smoothly flowing rivers dotted with islands" of chorale tunes. A choir dressed up to suggest the churchgoing fashion of the composer's time (but anachronistically including women), as well as a troupe of instrumentalists, aid in the effort to get beneath the skin of Bach's scores.

Epitomized here is another characteristic of the *Omnibus* appearances that will continue through the *Young People's Concerts*. It is easy to be misled by Alistair Cooke's allusion early on to "one man, a piano, and an orchestra," for these presentations called upon a whole panoply of staging devices and emerging tricks of the television-camera trade. There are costumes, lighting effects, and props ranging from simulated baseball diamonds (in a tonal composition "the tonic note is home plate") to scores, books, film clips, still pictures, and more. There is superimposition, cross-cutting, quick panning, zooming, and tilting as the art of using the television camera as an active participant in the filmed event rather than as just a passive witness grows more and more assured. Credit is due to *Omnibus* producer Robert Saudek, *Young People's Concerts* producer Roger Englander, and their numerous associates; their dynamism as well as Bernstein's is on display. Still, as writer, master of ceremonies, conductor, and sometimes soloist, Bernstein is clearly the focus of these programs.

Take as a contrasting instance of his mature style the *Young People's Concert* called "Musical Atoms: A Study of Intervals," broadcast November 29, 1965—a convenient glimpse also of the changes that had taken place in the public persona over the decade he had spent facing the camera. The hallmarks are all here: the down-to-earth metaphors and analogies (octaves on the keyboard are compared to the length of a foot on a measuring tape, and a passage of rising minor seconds is like "a great monster rising out of the sea"); the props (cards held up to enumerate intervals as they are played); the drawing on the familiar to elucidate the unfamiliar (the Beatles' "Help!" is played to illustrate the harmonic series). But the man delivering all this is an altered one. Many factors have operated on him over the course of a decade. Most significantly, perhaps, the fact that the *Young People's Concerts* series was taped before an audience, not made in an empty studio, cannot have failed to have its effect. Yet whatever accounts for it, at this mid-sixties juncture, in the heyday of his national esteem, we have full-fledged the eggheads' Johnny Carson, assured, even glib, totally at home before the camera.

And here too, when he mounts the podium to lead a movement of Vaughan Williams's Fourth Symphony, another widely known aspect of Bernstein's personality is in evidence: the conductor as mirror of the music. Feet wide apart as if braced against the onslaught of his own feelings, arms flailing, face contorted in effort and agony, hands clenched and shaking spastically, he mimes the music's progress—or, more precisely, embodies his reactions to its progress—at every important step. It is one more manifestation of the pedagogical urge: so anxious is he to drive home to his hearers the emotional grammar of the music he is conducting that he parses the musical sentence for them with grimace, gesture, and body English.

This tendency makes one of its earliest appearances in the aforementioned program on Bach, when Bernstein conducts a chorale sung at the moment of Christ's death in the *St. Matthew Passion*: eyes shut and shoulders hunched, he coaxes the music from the singers with fingers that seem to stroke the notes as they waft past him on the way to the microphones. It is noteworthy that this early example occurs when the only immediate onlooker is the camera. Professional musicians will declare that there is little need for graphic conductorial indications of what musical passages "mean" during a concert, for "meaning," along with fundamental matters such as whether a passage is to be played loudly or *very* loudly, are customarily worked out in rehearsals. But a camera pointed toward a virtually stationary figure on a podium, one that does almost nothing but wave a stick to indicate tempo, is not going to get much in the way of visual interest. It is conceivable that Bernstein's frequent encounters with the television camera consciously or unconsciously elicited the agitated podium style for which he is famous.

The *Young People's Concerts* were to continue through 1972, and considered as a whole, at least two remaining features of the series are remarkable. First is the breadth and catholicity of their content; Bernstein offers his fortunate audiences glimpses of everything from exotic musical instruments and concert-hall acoustics to the rudiments of scales, modes, forms, and orchestration; from Americanism and other varieties of nationalism in music to jazz and folk music in concert dress; from Bach and Beethoven to Stravinsky, Copland, Hindemith, and Mahler. Equally impressive is the array of musical talent the series, together with *Omnibus* and other earlier presentations, brought before the television cameras: Paul Tortelier, Jennie Tourel, Eileen Farrell, Stanley Drucker, Glenn Gould, Aaron Copland, Lynn Harrell, Shirley Verrett, Julius Baker, Christa Ludwig, Walter Berry, and Ralph Gomberg, to name just a few (as well as bringing such incidental pleasures as Carol Burnett's imitation of Ethel Merman in the *Omnibus* program on "American Musical Comedy").

With one notable exception—*The Unanswered Question*, the six Charles Eliot Norton lectures on musical linguistics that Bernstein delivered at Harvard in 1973—what has followed the *Young People's Concerts* bears much less of the personal Bernstein stamp. It mirrors his composing and conducting careers in various ways: of the former, for example, there is the tenth-anniversary Kennedy Center performance of his *Mass*, "A Theatre Piece for Singers, Players and Dancers" (1981), and other performances of his theatrical works, which make the transition from stage to television effectively but nonetheless remain second-generation to the medium; of the latter, a steady stream of televised symphonic performances encompassing many of the orchestral works of Beethoven and his opera *Fidelio*, all of the symphonies of Mahler, and a significant number of American works—the three nodes around which Bernstein's conducting career has pivoted since his departure from the stewardship of the New York Philharmonic in 1969. In many of these appearances he leads the Vienna Philharmonic or the Israel Philharmonic, the two orchestras with which he has been most closely identified over the past decade and a half.

Bernstein's television career began with Beethoven, and it will be no surprise if it closes on the same note. On the occasion of the bicentennial of Beethoven's birth in 1970, Bernstein made *Beethoven's Birthday: A Celebration in Vienna*, in which he acted multiply as host, tour guide, musical explicator, and conductor of portions of the master's First Piano Concerto (he leads from the keyboard) and *Fidelio*, and of the "Ode to Joy" from the Ninth Symphony. The program not only shows us what we might call the *doyen* Bernstein— and does so as well as anything since, I think, because shown at greater length—but also gives several twists to the thread that runs throughout his intellectual development as television reflects it: the universality of music.

The program deftly uses a format that has become familiar to audiences of the mid-eighties. The camera aerially pans the chosen locale, in this case Vienna's history-rich inner city, as the narrator's voice launches us into the subject at hand. Works of art, historical paintings and prints, restored architectural and cultural artifacts, and the like take us back to another time and introduce the principal characters of the historical drama. It could be any one of a hundred or more programs on our cultural and political past. Except for Bernstein: he quickly gets past the hackneyed view of Beethoven, telling us that his deafness "only reinforced an existing neurotic pattern," that the homely truth about his figure, so often shrouded by legend in nobility and forbearance, is that "nothing ever satisfied him," and that, contrary to what storybook tradition might suggest (to grownups), there is "a lack of evidence that he ever consummated his love affairs." A part of Beethoven, this latter-day advocate avers, never grew up. But the concomitant truth is that he was forever "a creature of grace and innocence and trust, even in his moments of greatest despair."

Now, Bernstein gets the typical engine going. "In this time of world hopelessness and agony and helplessness, we love his music and we need it. . . . This music is not only infinitely durable, but the closest music has ever come to universality. . . . That dubious cliché about music being the universal language almost comes true with Beethoven. No composer has ever lived who speaks so directly to so many people, to young and old, educated and ignorant, amateur and professional, sophisticated and naive." But it is more than Beethoven's reach that approaches the universal; the music itself is anchored in something essentially human. "This music bespeaks a universality of thought, of human brotherhood, freedom, and love."

Cliché or not, the notion of universality is one that pops up early in Bernstein's televised reflections on music and recurs often. In his programs about jazz and American musical comedy early in his career, he refuses to erect the artificial distinction between "art" music and vernacular music that characterized musical discourse both before and just after the Second World War. "Jazz is art," he declares boldly, and argues in effect that the characteristics commonly used to define and pigeonhole the phenomenon of music are superficial. As evidence he cites the fact that progressive jazz is coming to sound more and more like the "art" music of the time; musical comedy, for its part, tends more and more to resemble opera. Analogies again help to bridge the gaps created by superficial distinctions and to reveal hidden similarities. The *Singspiel*, that half-sung, half-spoken eighteenth-century theatrical genre, was "the *Annie Get Your Gun* of its day." To strip away the camouflage, "all we need is for our Mozart to come along. It could happen any second."

The underlying unity of all music extends beyond Western forms and styles. In a program on Japanese music he says, "It's always been the particular genius of the Japanese people to absorb elements from other cultures and then to assimilate them so deeply that they somehow re-emerge Japanese, just as the *gagaku* . . . was originally borrowed from China and Korea over a thousand years ago and then made into the official music of Japan."

The ultimate expression of Bernstein's hunt for universals is the televised Norton lectures at Harvard. Here he extends the pursuit beyond music to the links among all forms of human communication. He does so by means of a detailed and elaborately illustrated series of translations of the terms of Noam Chomsky's structural linguistics into musical equivalents. He proceeds from phonology to syntax to semantics, finding musical analogues for Chomsky's linguistic "deep structure" as he goes. When he has finished creating his tools, he uses them to diagnose the nature of the twentieth century's musical crisis: the disintegration of tonality and the fragmentation of stylistic coherence. Ultimately his search for "a worldwide, inborn musical grammar" leads him where we might expect: to the notion that a great saving musical synthesis is at hand. "We have reached that supra-level of abstract musical semantics, of pure Idea, where those apparently mismatched components can unite—tonal, nontonal, electronic, serial, aleatory—all united in a magnificent new eclecticism. But this electronic union can take place only if all the elements are combined with and embedded in the tonal universe—that is, conceived against a contextual background of tonality."

Utilizing, like the early *Omnibus* shows, a variety of visual aids, props, and musical examples by both solo piano and orchestra, the Norton lectures have a dual significance in the context of Bernstein's career: they are both an embodiment of a lifelong personal odyssey of mind and spirit and a demonstration of the power and versatility of television as a pedagogical medium. The quest for universals seems to have been fulfilled—or at least to have achieved a state of quiescence. It is television's privilege to have been not just a passive observer of Bernstein's quest but an active partner.

Leonard Bernstein: Video Man

by HUMPHREY BURTON

THE catalogue of Leonard Bernstein films and videotapes goes back more than thirty years. His early work on CBS—the *Omnibus* series and the shows sponsored by Ford and Lincoln—remains the most distinguished, the most entertaining, and the most influential body of analytical programs about music ever made. People over fifty still talk with nostalgic excitement about the way Lenny had the orchestra spread out on a studio floor painted to represent a page of the orchestral score; about the famous jazz players who helped with his exposition of different styles to answer the question "What is jazz?"; about the essay on *La Bohème* ("What makes opera grand?"), which had actors speaking separately the lines subsequently *sung* together in the Quartet from Act III; about his illuminating essay on the technique of conducting, in which he took the first page of Brahms's First Symphony as his text. There were, in all, twenty-five of these stimulating programs—and they were for adults, a rarity then and unheard of these days.

More than once I have tried to persuade him to remake some of the shows with 1980s techniques, including color and stereo, but Lenny is adamant—they were the programs of a young man, he says, impossible for him to deliver all over again in his late sixties. But at least a selection of the scripts remains in book form as a beacon for program-makers around the world. The first book was entitled *The Joy of Music*, the second *The Infinite Variety of Music*, and both should be on every music lover's bookshelf.

Humphrey Burton is the former head of Music and Arts for the BBC. His long association with Bernstein began when he produced the BBC's arts magazine *Monitor*. He is now artistic director of London's Barbican Centre and has been associated with Tanglewood's Seventieth Birthday Gala Celebration for Leonard Bernstein.

*Bernstein conducting the Vienna Philharmonic in Beethoven on
a live-in-concert film, 1970*

Bernstein's *Young People's Concerts* represent a second period of television activity, equally important, from an educational standpoint, for more than a decade. There were no less than fifty-three programs in all, and it's a pity they are not available on home video or cable TV, because they are a lot of fun.

But around 1970, after Bernstein relinquished conductorship of the New York Philharmonic, there was a major shift in emphasis, both geographically and in terms of content. For the Beethoven bicentenary in 1970, Bernstein went to Vienna, where he conducted *Fidelio* in Beethoven's *Theater-an-der-Wien* and around the performance made *Beethoven's Birthday* for CBS, an Emmy-winning "special," which was also notable for being an anniversary show transmitted a year late by the American network.

Vienna has since been the center of Bernstein's film activities. With the Vienna Philharmonic he has recorded four major symphonic cycles. First came all the symphonies of Mahler (except the Second, filmed in Ely Cathedral with the London Symphony Orchestra, and *Das Lied von der Erde*, made with the Israel Philharmonic in Tel Aviv). Next came the Beethoven symphonies, then Brahms, and most recently Schumann, all filmed on thirty-five millimeter with stereo sound.

The Unitel production company in Munich has invested substantial sums in these productions. Each public concert in Vienna is filmed twice, with Deutsche Grammophon recording the sound digitally. Bernstein insists on doing everything "live," so even the retakes are done with an audience. Each concert uses as much film stock as a feature film, with as many as six blimped Arriflex cameras running all through the concert. Close-up pictures of individual instruments are filmed later in a small studio with the players miming to the played-back sound of the concert recording.

Quite apart from deciding what to look at with the six cameras placed strategically in and around the orchestra, the director has the mind-boggling task of organizing the script so that each camera can change its film magazine in turn three or four times in each symphony. By comparison, television production seems like child's play, and rather less intrusive for the public in the hall; however, the wider range of camera angles and the precision cutting offered by film make it the preferred method, despite the heat of the film lights and the occasional clunk of soundproofed cameras being unlocked preparatory to reloading.

All this said, the present writer has what Mr. Bernstein might label a "sneaky feeling" that among the most satisfying Bernstein video concerts have been live occasions televised on tape. Notable in the 1970s were two splendid London concerts with the London Symphony Orchestra: the Verdi *Requiem* from St. Paul's Cathedral (1970) and the Stravinsky Memorial Concert from the Royal Albert Hall (1972). From the 1980s, I recall with special pleasure a Haydn Mass performed in the magnificent basilica at Ottobeuren in Bavaria one sun-soaked summer afternoon and a superb Bartók-Schumann concert televised live from Budapest.

For Leonard Bernstein, music is surely a form of theater. As a director, I see my job as a form of theatrical presentation, and nothing could be more dramatic, more intense, than his reading of Verdi's *Requiem*. It is truly a joy and privilege to work with Bernstein in the service of music.

As a postscript, the following is an edited account of Mr. Bernstein's memories of the pioneer days.

I've been through music on television for a long time—since the earliest days, the fifties, when I did a great deal of work with those wonderful pioneers Robert Saudek and Mary Ahern and later with Roger Englander.

In those days it was *live* live. There were no teleprompters and you had one shot at it. There was no such thing as videotape. And if I did a ninety-minute show, on what was then called *Omnibus*, I jolly well had to memorize ninety minutes of script and music, and remember at what point I went to the piano or to the podium or crossed to the microphone or to the blackboard or whatever. And I used to stay up nights, not just writing it but memorizing. I remember my wife Felicia hearing my lines and falling asleep, and then Adolph Green would come over and spell her—one would take a nap while the other one heard me. Those were tough days, and whatever went out on the air, that's what people heard and saw—and if there were mistakes, there were mistakes!

I remember one of the early *Omnibus* shows, "The Art of Conducting," in which I drew a blank, I dried. I was standing in the middle of this huge studio having not a clue as to what the next thought or sentence was. I've seen a kinescope of it. I really just stand there and shuffle and kick and scratch my nose and pretend to cough; I take my handkerchief and wipe off the perspiration and sort of hem and haw like somebody in the House of Lords. I think I finally wandered over to the piano where there was a cue sheet pasted underneath somewhere where the camera couldn't see it, and had a look. But watching the kinescope there seems like an eternity. There must have been a good forty seconds of dead air, which would never be permitted these days. So I've been through the hard ways and the easy ways, and the point is that it is all hard. But I know the ups and the downs, and I would say offhand that the ups far outweigh the downs.

The great benefit, for me, is the educational value, not only in the pedagogical sense but in the best sense of acquainting people with new stuff they can come to love (which is what I mean by education, rather than having to memorize the conjugation of an irregular verb). Bringing music close to people: as you know that has always been my lifelong desire and goal even in writing my own music. And I think there is nothing that comes near to television for this purpose. This is the best communicative means, and, after all, communication is what television is about.

Talking About Music:
The Maestro and the Masses
OR
Reflections of a Child of the Sixties

by D. KERN HOLOMAN

LEONARD BERNSTEIN and I have never met, I think, though our paths have crossed frequently enough that it's possible we've shaken hands in a green room somewhere. Yet in some ways his career has been quite simply the dominant influence on my own, and that being so I can't help wondering whether he hasn't molded many of the fundamental attitudes toward good music held by what is now called the television generation. Before the compact disc, the video-tape, and the Walkman, after all, there was Lenny. For those of us who were born, raised, and educated far from the Boston-New York corridor the efforts of Leonard Bernstein were central to classical music's having become a major force in our lives. I'll bet there's a little of the maestro in virtually every child of the sixties who went on to have a career in American music-making.

It began, of course, with the televised *Omnibus* programs and the *Young People's Concerts*, of which I am told there were some five dozen in the late fifties and sixties. These followed, in my family, reverent attention to the Toscanini radio broadcasts (I remember especially a Verdi Requiem from my earliest childhood, perhaps from the Met on Holy Saturday, when our household came to an unaccustomed standstill); and the fifteen-minute broadcasts of Benjamin

D. Kern Holoman is a musicologist and orchestral conductor at the University of California, Davis. His book *Berlioz* will appear shortly from Harvard University Press.

Swalin and the North Carolina Symphony, every Wednesday at eleven forty-five during my primary years at school in Raleigh, N.C. But television was different: you could see what had theretofore lived only in the mind's eye, and the attractions far outdistanced the drawbacks.

I don't recall the repertoire of the television programs especially well: Bach and Beethoven and Mozart and Mahler, I should think, for I remember learning about these composers from television. What was captivating at the time was the way the Maestro played his excerpts at the piano, then turned to conduct the orchestra—now, say, in the Allegretto from Beethoven's Seventh, a minute later in Tchaikovsky's *Romeo and Juliet*. I wondered how they managed it, and began to think in broad terms about the conductor as producer. I admired, too, the many young soloists, not so much older than I, who came to be on these programs; I saw something of the competition that lay ahead. I would hang on his every word, and try to understand.

Leonard Bernstein called this exercise "talking about music"— talking, as he put it, "with friends, colleagues, teachers, students, and just plain simple citizens." You will read in your *New Grove* that "these numerous national television appearances . . . brought him enormous popularity," or, as *Baker's Biographical Dictionary* has it, that "these concerts obtained wide popularity, not confined solely to the eponymous youth."

But the word popularity is hardly sufficient to describe the effect he had on the prepubescent band-and-orchestra set. We were, I would say, seduced: by his undeniable good looks, the suave patrician accent, the seeming inexhaustability of his talents and powers. His "talking about music" seemed grace itself, and in that respect he taught us what good music teaching was long before we encountered university-level courses in musical grammar and history. We learned, in our early teens, of form and structure and harmony; we began to think about "meaning in music." Somewhere in there Santa Claus brought the household a copy of Bernstein's *Joy of Music*, and in some very vivid ways this book first introduced me to the concept, not just of "talking about music," but of writing about it as well.

It's worth going back to read *The Joy of Music* (1954). What strikes you about the prose is how inherently sensible it is, and how little things have changed. "There is a human urge to clarify, rationalize, justify, analyze, limit, describe," Bernstein writes. "There is also a great urge to 'sell' music, arising out of the transformation of music in the last two hundred years into an industry. Suddenly there are mass markets, a tremendous recording industry, professional careerists, civic competitiveness, music chambers of commerce." Out of this, he says, has come what Virgil Thomson called the "Music Appreciation Racket":

> It is, in the main, a racket, because it is in the main specious and commercial. It uses every device to sell music: cajoling, coyness, flattery, oversimplification, irrelevant entertainment, tall tales—all in order to keep the music business booming. And in so doing it has itself become a business. The next step is obviously a new parasitic development—music-appreciation appreciation.

Strong words, these, and surprisingly apt today, though I think we've made some progress, overall, in dismissing second-rate critical attitudes from our musical discourse. (Program and record-jacket notes have much improved in the last decade; there's relatively little of what Bernstein calls the birds-bees-and-rivulets sort of commentary.) Plenty of solid instruction is crammed into *The Joy of Music*; the rudiments of music appreciation—elementary acoustics, a little harmony, some counterpoint, the Tristan chord—are all there. Tucked in with the rudiments comes, moreover, a pretty fair grasp of Beethoven sketch study and of Baroque performance practice, two areas of music scholarship that were then still in their adolescence. Not to mention Mahler and Berlioz. Virgil Thomson is right to say that few have ever presented such material "so warmly, so sincerely, so skillfully. As musical mind-openers they are first class; as pedagogy they are matchless."

Much the same could be said of *The Infinite Variety of Music* (1959) and of Bernstein's Charles Eliot Norton lectures at Harvard in 1973, published as *The Unanswered Question* (1976). This latter represents the maestro's wide-eyed, innocent, and pleasingly naive romp through his favorite repertoire subsequent to his discovering Chomskian linguistic principles. It culminates in a *credo* of devastating implications: "I believe that from [the] Earth emerges a musical poetry, which is by the nature of its sources tonal." But whatever you care to make of the central thesis—and it is not popular in the sorts of places I work—you have to admire the scope of the campaign, the military precision with which he marshals his forces, and the complexity of the field of battle, which in this case was Harvard, the

BSO, and the old *Young People's Concerts* all rolled into one. You want to have been there.

Still in the early sixties, Leonard Bernstein managed to hurl two more formative thunderbolts in my direction. In March 1961, Bernstein and the New York Philharmonic appeared on our local concert series. The program was to open with the overture to something called *Candide*. I had taken enough interest in the title to have found a copy of the Voltaire in my father's study, and I carried the volume, as ostentatiously as I could manage, to the concert. I was prepared for little else that followed: not for the lilting excitement of the music, nor for the romance of the very idea of a composer-conductor. Nor for what I vividly remember as a silvery aura about the maestro as he worked (a follow-spot?), nor for the sounds coming from what we assumed to be the best orchestra in the world. A classmate and I had ascertained where his dressing room was to be found, and during the intermission we hung around outside, not to collect an autograph, but simply to see this legend close up. I like to think he smiled in our general direction. It was that night, I'm almost certain, that I resolved to become an orchestra conductor myself.

The first stereophonic recording I purchased was a New York Philharmonic performance of Brahms's Fourth (1963). I bought it not so much to hear the work, which I did not know, as to hear music in stereo and to examine the fine photograph, on the jacket, of the orchestra in its splendid new Philharmonic Hall. There was much here to attract a budding bassoonist, not least of all the lifting, in the picture, of the woodwind and brass into prominence on risers. The symphony, of course, was haunting. Brahms IV was the work that sustained me through the most ghastly days of early double-reed playing.

I suppose Leonard Bernstein had become, to provincials of my generation, what is now called a role model. It wasn't his stature with the "beautiful people" of New York, about which we knew little and cared less, nor the dawn of the jet-set conductor, which in some respects we took as a matter of course. It was the easy and encyclopedic command of so many avenues of music-making. ("Ebullient," says *Baker's*, "with multifarious talents.") We saw a bold candor about things that we much admired, a courage of conviction, a naked and compelling love of music that was always erupting in the most memorable of fashions. It didn't hurt to see him embrace political ideals that we were beginning to hold especially dear.

We grew apart after that, the Maestro to his composition and I to my musicology. Ultimately the mystique of another composer-conductor, Hector Berlioz, took precedence in my imagination and became the focus of my work. Our itineraries converged again at a Berlioz festival in Paris, which was to conclude with Bernstein's conducting the Requiem in the church of the Invalides. A boyhood friend of mine (who had since had the misfortune of finding himself in the very first college class I ever taught) had become an assistant to the man I now learned to think of as "Mr. B." He fed me the Maestro's schedule, and I took advantage of that information to steal into the rehearsals. Safe in the comfort of my new Ph.D. degree and a good job in the Best of All Possible Worlds, I went, I'm sure, to catch this formidable performing force in some musicological *bêtise*. Instead I found myself there behind a column in the Invalides as hypnotized as I had been by *Candide* in North Carolina more than a decade before. The ecstasy with which the Maestro worked the musicians, and the fire with which they responded—to say nothing of the unruly coiffure—had much to say of Berlioz himself.

Now, having reached forty just as the Maestro reaches seventy, I have conducting students of my own, and together we play and replay a videotape of Beethoven's Ninth with Bernstein and the Vienna Philharmonic, watching for exactly how he does this or that. We watch a lot of other conductors, too, but somehow it's Bernstein's Beethoven Ninth we have watched most closely over the years.

But this was to be less an autobiographical cameo than an essay on the spell of television. It was to have been a look at the pressing issue of how art music reaches the public. For every working musician of today is faced with the problem of how to offer learned but comprehensible discourse about music to those who pay our bills. This issue is the more urgent as the matter of audience renewal becomes in many circles a clear and urgent necessity of life. As Michael Steinberg has put it, "the opportunity to help people find a way into a difficult musical experience—perhaps intrinsically and permanently difficult, perhaps difficult only because of unfamiliarity—is more than an opportunity. It is an obligation."

"The public is not a great beast," Bernstein writes, "but an intelligent organism, more often than not longing for insight and knowledge. . . . There is, after all, a common meeting ground for the writer and the musician." (There is even room for some romance: "If we add to all this the God-given human capacity for association, there is no reason to carp at the spectacle of a simple Lyric Poet indulging himself a little sentimentally in a metaphor of hills and Beethoven.") And contemporary mass media, as Bernstein has shown, offer us inexhaustible opportunities for "talking about music," and on a scale the implications of which we have just begun to understand.

So nowadays I conduct a little and "talk about music" a great deal: to scholars, to students, and to the public, and I enjoy each of these constituencies just as much as the others. Talking about music to the general public has its particular attractions, as when an Old Aggie recently told me, at intermission, that he had heard the first and second groups in the exposition all right, but it seemed like there was no development before the recapitulation. He was right.

As it happens, I was led not so long ago to talk about Leonard Bernstein as composer. "He is a prodigious, multi-talented American musician," I began, "an omniscient presence on the American musical scene." I went on to perorate:

> Bernstein is arguably the most successful composer-conductor since Mahler. He has, moreover, been able to bridge, with uncanny vision, the traditional chasm between the appeal of popular music and the rigor of classical idioms. . . . It has been voguish in some circles to regard Bernstein as too fluent and quick for his own good, a victim of his too-easy control of too many parameters of professional music-making. I believe, however, that his accomplishments make him an intellectual giant and a model to be emulated. The truth is that few enough American musicians have enjoyed his artistic stature or matched his breadth of genius, and the nation's musical establishment is the healthier for his efforts.

I am a fan, and proud of it. When I grow up, I should like to be, let's say, half so good.

Sketch for the piano-vocal score of the Gospel of Mass: "God said, Let there be rats," 1972, lyrics by Stephen Schwartz

7

International Celebrity

Bernstein has been active on the international scene from very early in his career. He has maintained a close relationship with the Israel Philharmonic Orchestra since 1947 and was the first American to conduct an opera at La Scala, where he led Cherubini's Medea—with Maria Callas in the title role—in another of those dramatic last-minute replacements for an ailing conductor (for La Scala he learned the opera in a matter of days). He conducts regularly in London, Munich, Paris, and all the other great musical centers of Europe.

But there is one European city that has welcomed him almost as a native son, where his works have been performed frequently (and often to greater critical acclaim than they receive in the United States), where his performances as a conductor are instantly sold out, and where he himself is a celebrity of movie-star proportions. This city, oddly enough, is the old, reserved, and occasionally ethnocentric capital of the Austro-Hungarian Empire, the home of great composers (most of whom were born elsewhere), the metropolis on the not-very-blue Danube: Vienna.

Lenny's Vienna

by MARCEL PRAWY

AUSTRIANS have a deep conviction that it was in Vienna, the capital on the Danube, that Leonard Bernstein was discovered. You might be inclined to say: "What nerve! Haven't they ever heard of those American debuts in 1943 and 1944?" But the Viennese are persistent in their conviction. Their past record of discovery is far better than popular history will admit. While the undeniable difficulties that have faced certain composers there have received worldwide attention, Vienna was nonetheless the first international city to embrace Wagner, Bruckner, and Mahler. As far as our Maestro Bernstein is concerned, Vienna immediately understood his message. The routine commonplaces of Bernsteinology are rejected in Vienna: "Amazing how many different things one man can do. . . ." It's all so different in Vienna.

Suppose you are in Paris, New York, or London, and you would like to find out whether Mr. Bernstein is in town (by the way, nobody calls him that—it's "Lenny" or "the Maestro"). How would you go about it? Probably by inquiring from the musical organization that is presenting him. Superfluous in Vienna! Here one *knows*. Groups gather around the hotel. People who would never normally meet during the year meet one another. Semi-strangers may ask each other: "Are you going to the rehearsal?" No need to specify which work, which hall, what hour. One knows that something is in the air.

I remember one day in 1966 when there was a recording session of a Mozart concerto in Schoenbrunn Palace, with Leonard Bernstein

The Vienna State Opera's director of education, Marcel Prawy has written widely about the history of Vienna and its operatic institutions and has translated many Broadway shows for production in German-speaking countries.

as pianist and conductor of the Vienna Philharmonic Orchestra. Technical problems forced an extended break. The Maestro remained at the piano and began to warm up. Soon he started to improvise: Mozart, Wagner, Beethoven, Bernstein, Gershwin, Joplin, and finally the waltz from *Der Rosenkavalier*. The musicians—only those needed for the Mozart concerto were on hand—strode in, took out their instruments, and joined in, one by one. The glory of Viennese Baroque architecture shone upon that "Bernsteinized" version of Viennese twentieth-century rococo music, improvised by a genius with a loving group of musicians.

Vienna is of the opinion that the 1943 explosion of Bernstein's career in the United States was due to the birth of a genius at the right time. America at war needed a brilliant young native son to encourage the artistic morale by giving a national counterpart to the "-ninis, -owskis, and -inskis that abounded on the international scene." The Maestro was twenty-nine when he first conducted the Vienna Symphony Orchestra at the *Konzerthaus* in 1948. But the real Viennese explosion came in 1966, when he conducted *Falstaff*, staged by Lucchino Visconti, at the *Staatsoper*.

Vienna's love affair with the Maestro started with *Der Rosenkavalier*—a new production (1968) of this most Viennese of all operas, staged by the most Viennese of all stage directors, Otto Schenk, at the *Staatsoper*. Was it really necessary, some people asked themselves, to engage an American to teach our musicians how to play Richard Strauss? Gloom was predicted for the rehearsals. But he came and worked on an unusual cello decrescendo in the prelude to the Italian singer's aria and on previously uninterpreted nuances in the waltz. Total authority was established at once; total love followed soon thereafter. The climax came when he worked with the cast on diction: Christa Ludwig from Berlin, Reri Grist from New York, Gwyneth Jones from Wales, even Walter Berry (the only Viennese)—all accepted Leonard Bernstein's suggestions for correct "Wienerisch."

Leonard Bernstein and Vienna, reciprocal love. The hundredth anniversary of our State Opera building was celebrated in 1969 with the Vienna Philharmonic Orchestra and the Vienna State Opera Chorus in a Bernstein Beethoven concert. The two-hundredth anniversary of Beethoven's birth followed in 1970 with a new production of *Fidelio* under the Maestro, again staged by Otto Schenk, at the

Theater an der Wien, where the work had had its world premiere in 1805. How many discussions did we have about the final *G* of the G-major duet between Leonore and Florestan, which Bernstein conducted without a pause into the opening *G* of the following *Leonore No. 3* Overture!

Bernstein's pilgrimages to the places where Mozart, Beethoven, and Mahler lived are a familiar sight in our city. But I believe there is no one on earth who really knows Leonard Bernstein's true depths behind all the widely publicized commercial glamor. I envy anyone who has the courage to write his biography. One day while in Vienna he had retired from one of his late-night parties rather early and told us he had to prepare a script for a telecast on Sigmund Freud to be taped early the following morning. Some wise guy remarked that he might be going off to some bar with a circle of closer friends for a few more drinks. Maybe he did—but the next morning at nine o'clock sharp, there he was in front of Sigmund Freud's house on the *Burggasse* with a script in his own handwriting, which he delivered live before the TV cameras in German. I heard him make the most interesting comments on the development of American jazz after a Beethoven concert during a party at the U.S. ambassador's residence, where he sat on the lawn surrounded by fans. The most interesting explications of Beethoven came at 3 a.m. in the Viennese jazz club "Atrium." An amazing man! You never leave him without a phrase, a word, a thought that will stick in your head for a lifetime.

In 1968 I narrated a concert version of Meyerbeer's opera *Les Huguenots* and mentioned to the Maestro that during my narration I suddenly felt how similar this story was to *Romeo and Juliet*, to *West Side Story*: Catholics and Protestants, Puerto Ricans and New Yorkers, Raoul and Valentine, Tony and Maria. Lenny: "There is only one story: everybody hates everybody and two people are in love!" I will never forget this answer.

It seemed natural to us that he celebrated his sixtieth birthday in Vienna—to be absolutely correct, at Wolf Trap in Vienna, Virginia, close to Washington, D.C. By the way, in Austria there is a town called Bernstein, but, unfortunately, of no relation!

I do not think there is any place of importance in Vienna that Leonard Bernstein has not distinguished by his conducting: the *Staatsoper* and the *Theater an der Wien*, the *Musikverein* and the *Konzerthaus*, the multi-purpose giant called the *Stadthalle*. He conducted the Vienna Philharmonic Orchestra Ball and recorded at the *Sophien-säle*, where Johann Strauss once made the Viennese dance.

Lenny's Vienna! Among the crowd attending the opening of the John F. Kennedy Center for the Performing Arts in Washington—and the premiere of Bernstein's *Mass*—in 1970 were three Viennese: Rudolf Gamsjäger, then general manager-designate of the *Staatsoper*, Leopold Gratz, then minister of education, and myself, in Washington to celebrate my transfer from the *Volksoper* to the managerial staff of the *Staatsoper*. I vividly recall the excitement in the new hall, the public comments on the architecture and the dresses, and the questions everyone posed: Would President Nixon attend? Would Jackie Kennedy? At the end, an enthusiastic audience greeted the composer and counted the kisses he bestowed on a splendid cast of youngsters. Afterward they rushed to a glamorous reception in the new building. Mixed reviews followed the next day, but Gamsjäger whispered into my ear, after listening to about thirty minutes of Bernstein's most underrated work: "We will produce it at the Vienna State Opera!" As it turned out, Vienna first saw a guest performance of *Mass* by the Yale Symphony Orchestra in English, brought to the *Konzerthaus* by General Manager Peter Weiser. The State Opera production in my German translation followed in 1981 under General Manager Egon Seefehlner. Rave reviews, sold-out houses, and well-deserved cheers greeted this masterpiece, which held its place in the repertory alternating with the standard operatic classics. The Vienna State Opera is proud that it remains the only major opera house in the world to give this piece its overdue prestige, surrounded by works of Mozart, Wagner, and Strauss.

By 1981, Vienna had already become the world capital of Bernsteinland. I am deeply proud that the entire theatrical output of Leonard Bernstein was first produced on the European continent by me in my German translation. Americans show a strange mixture of superiority and inferiority complexes, both in the wrong places. An undeserved inferiority complex belittles the American musical theater as pure entertainment, as something merely transient. Europeans seem to understand its true importance far better and have included the major American works in the permanent repertory of their opera houses.

Vienna's attachment to the musical theater of Leonard Bernstein began with my production of *Wonderful Town* at the *Volksoper* in

Bernstein joins the Viennese cast of Mass *for the curtain call after the first performance at the Staatsoper*

The Vienna Staatsoper, with a large screen set up to broadcast Bernstein's performance of his Kaddish Symphony *(given in commemoration of the fortieth anniversary of the atomic*

*bombing of Hiroshima) to accommodate the crowd that could
not obtain tickets for the performance inside, August 1985*

1956, before Bernstein's personal impact had shaken our town. We were the first ones on the European continent to produce *West Side Story*—in 1968, at the *Volksoper*, at the same time the Maestro was conducting *Der Rosenkavalier* at the *Staatsoper*. If we had not produced this work, others surely would have—but for nine years after its world premiere, in 1957, nobody on our continent dared to try it. While *West Side Story* is a smash hit wherever it is shown, it was in Vienna—the so-called tradition-minded capital—that everyone understood they had witnessed a modern rebirth of the popular opera of bygone days, a modern equivalent of such beloved pieces as *La Bohème* or *La Traviata*, which become immortal by veiling laughter and tears, love and hatred, life and death, in a velvet gown of beautiful melodies. "*Sempre libera*" and "I feel pretty," "*Che gelida manina*" and "Tonight." We did our share in trying to salvage the glorious music of *Candide* from the chains of a burdensome libretto. Soon after the world premiere, I produced a German concert version of the entire original score for the Austrian Broadcasting System. Later Harold Prince brought his novel mini-version to the *Stadthalle*.

A funny pre-planned incident happened during the Carinthian Summer Festival, at a concert devoted to Bernstein's symphonic works. Harry Kraut, the Maestro's friend, partner, impresario, and alter ego, had pointed out that legal entanglements would prevent the Maestro from conducting. The Budapest National Orchestra was performing under the late Janos Ferencsik, but we knew that the Maestro could not stand certain interpretations of the *Candide* overture. He attended the rehearsals—and at the concert conducted the overture as an encore!

The symphonic works of the Maestro are frequently played in Vienna. The premiere of the latest edition of the *Kaddish* Symphony took place at a Bernstein festival produced by the Carinthian Summer Festival. It was later performed at the State Opera under the composer's baton in the Hiroshima Peace Concert of 1985 and was watched in a telecast by millions.

Only Vienna did full justice to the opera *A Quiet Place*, which had taken such a critical beating in the United States. We produced it at the Vienna State Opera in English (after La Scala of Milan), with the composer conducting. The public response was splendid, and the critics gave unanimous approval—in both cities. The most obnoxious of all critical objections against the Maestro's serious music, the word "eclectic," is no invective to our ears. We love melody. In Vienna, we simply adore good eclectic music. It has a legitimate place in the modern musical world, just like the avant garde. Happy Birthday, dear Maestro. And thank you for everything you have given us to enrich our lives.

Changing John F. Kennedy's famous saying, your message to us means: "*Ich bin ein Wiener.*"

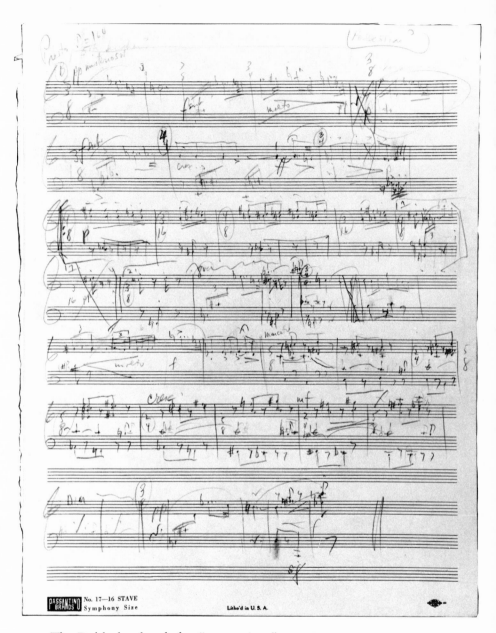

The Dybbuk, *sketch for "possession,"* 1972

8

Conductor

From the very beginning Leonard Bernstein's conducting attracted attention—not always because of his interpretations. Often it was his nervous, athletic, even driven, style of beating (or stamping or swaying or nodding his head or otherwise signaling the mood of the music) that attracted attention and was argued by critics, pro and con. He has been accused of carefully calculating these gestures not for the benefit of the orchestra playing the notes, but to signal to the audience what they should be hearing in the performance (a view contradicted by many who have attended private rehearsals or recording sessions, in which no audience is present to receive signals).

Such discussions have often overlooked the result of the performances, obtained through painstaking—and often endless, or seemingly endless—rehearsal. But almost any musician who has played under his direction can recall particular concerts that remain highlights in his or her musical experience for the combination of musical insight, passion, willingness to re-study and re-think scores from the ground up, energy, and that particular indefinable spark that, in the end, makes things happen.

Britten—a Rollicking Round

by PHYLLIS CURTIN

IN 1946, with a couple of semesters of Boris Goldovsky's opera course at the New England Conservatory behind me, I auditioned for the opera program at Tanglewood and was accepted. In almost no time, it seemed, Mildred Miller, mezzo-soprano, and I were assigned the roles of Nieces 1 and 2 in *Peter Grimes*, and we took up residence—or very nearly—in the Theater-Concert Hall. All the roles, I believe, were double cast, save for ours, we thus had double rehearsals of every scene we were in. I remember being marvelously happy and little else about the rehearsals and performances, except one thing—Lenny's rehearsing, *teaching* us all, cast and chorus, to sing the great rollicking 7/4 chorus, "Old Joe has gone fishing." Certainly every musician who knows Lenny will appreciate how much this particular rhythm went to his fancy, his feet, his humor. Nothing was ever more sheerly exhilarating to prepare. We danced it and laughed it, and how wonderfully we sang it!

A couple of decades later I sang Ellen Orford in performances celebrating Britten at the Edinburgh Festival and later at the Met. I always longed for Lenny's "Old Joe." None ever came near to living the necessity of that song as Lenny did.

I've shared many thrilling performances with Lenny, whose heartbeats are always there to sing with—as in the glorious *Missa solemnis* at Tanglewood on the twentieth anniversary of Koussevitzky's death. Perhaps "Old Joe" prepared me for living Lenny's music-making, no matter what the score.

Phyllis Curtin, dean of Boston University's School of the Arts, enjoyed a distinguished career as operatic and concert singer; she has long been a distinguished teacher of singing formerly at Yale and the Aspen School of Music, currently at Boston University and Tanglewood.

Mahler: With Bernstein in Israel

by CAROL LIEBERMAN

W HEN I joined the violin section of the Israel Philharmonic in 1967, Leonard Bernstein had already been associated with the orchestra for twenty years, since he first appeared with them in 1947. It is difficult to convey in words the special relationship that existed between Bernstein and the members of the IPO, or why one performance of Mahler's First Symphony should still linger in my mind as the greatest orchestral experience of my life. Perhaps some background might help to illuminate the situation as it was back in those days.

In 1967, the membership of the IPO was still composed largely of immigrants, many of whom had fled Hitler. These were consummate musicians who had achieved the highest degree of artistic refinement in the cultural centers of Germany and Austria, as well as in the *stetls* of Russia and Poland. They had suffered unspeakable degradation and personal tragedy and, upon coming to what was then Palestine, had worked as cab drivers, as laborers, or at any other job just to survive. In addition to these senior players, there were several young *sabras*, or native-born Israelis, and about ten percent American or younger foreign-born musicians. The basic character and playing style of the orchestra was central European, which meant that there was a slight delay in response to the beat of the conductor's baton. It took a bit of getting used to for an American trained to play immediately after the beat!

The IPO was also unique in that it was run entirely as a cooperative. A committee drawn from the membership, along with the

---

Violinist Carol Lieberman performs regularly on modern and period violins; she is an assistant professor of music at the College of the Holy Cross.

artistic director, Zubin Mehta, made the decisions concerning repertoire as well as guest conductors. And since Mehta was actually in residence only about two months during the season, guest conductors came at the rate of one every three or four weeks. In this tiny country of three million people, five or six performances a week were not unusual. In addition to the heavy performing schedule, the concert halls presented their own special challenges as well. There was the luxurious Mann Auditorium in Tel Aviv, where the orchestra made its home, and where the majority of concerts were held. But there was also the monthly series of concerts that took place in a beat-up old movie theater in Haifa, where shells from sunflower seeds littered the floors (despite the presence of signs forbidding the "spitting of shells" in the movie theater!) and where no orchestra member wanted to sit toward the outside for fear of falling off the tiny stage.

Given the varied backgrounds, the day-to-day frustrations of life in Israel, and the fact that the seat of power was much closer to the membership than is customary, it was not surprising that emotions were often close to the surface. It was a difficult task for any but the great conductors to impose discipline under these circumstances. For such eminent masters as Claudio Abbado, Carlo Maria Giulini, and Josef Krips (who terrified many of the younger players), the orchestra was always on its best behavior. Other conductors not quite in that league did not fare nearly as well.

But there was one conductor whose presence seemed to change the very air that people breathed, and that was "Lenny." When Lenny came, it was an event. He was family! Here was a conductor who understood Yiddish and Hebrew, and who could and did argue Talmud with the best of them. Perhaps equally important, here was a conductor who was just as emotional and volatile as they were. Lenny did not simply greet orchestra members, he embraced them, he kissed them, and they responded in turn. During rehearsals, everything was said and done on a personal level: the intensity was palpable, and the decibel level was high.

I was frankly awestruck by Bernstein. When I was growing up in New York City, it had been Leonard Bernstein's voice that came over the radio bringing us his *Young People's Concerts*. I don't think that any programming for young people before or since then has come close to the imagination and innovation of those concerts. How different Bernstein's warmth and accessibility seemed from the other voice of greatness that came over the airways: Arturo Toscanini. We

Bernstein conducting the Palestine Philharmonic Orchestra in his
Jeremiah *Symphony with mezzo-soprano Edith Goldschmidt*
(Dhel Theater, Tel-Aviv, April 29, 1947)

could hear the venerable patriarch in rehearsal with the NBC Symphony berating the musicians in his relentless quest to realize the composer's intentions. They seemed at opposite poles, Lenny and the great Toscanini. It was youth versus age; the young Massachusetts native pitting himself against the formidable cultural domination of the Europeans embodied in "The Maestro." There was Toscanini, product of the great nineteenth-century traditions, a cellist in Verdi's own orchestra. And here was Lenny, an American, equally at home in "pop" and jazz idioms, a Harvard graduate who wrote his senior thesis on nationalism in American music and the origins of jazz. And also, by way of contrast, Bernstein's conducting was demonstrative and subjective. He did not attempt to submerge his ego in order to convey the meaning of the music; rather, he channelled the music through his own personality, and with equally stunning results.

Perhaps this is what has helped make Bernstein such a great interpreter of Mahler. Certainly they have much in common. Both were sons of self-made Jewish businessmen, and both became self-made musicians. Both Mahler and Bernstein were gifted pianists before turning to composition and conducting. Both are drawn to dramatic music and theatrical productions, and both are able to synthesize in their compositions the seemingly disparate elements in folk and popular themes with Western art music. Both write program music closely allied with song, and both remain firmly rooted in the major/minor tonal systems, despite the more radical compositional styles around them. Certainly other parallels may be drawn, but at the root of them all is the sheer emotional intensity of both Mahler and Bernstein, which seems at times to strain the boundaries of "good taste," but never oversteps them.

Just as Mahler and Bernstein seem spiritual partners, so it was in 1967 with Mahler and the Israel Philharmonic. Mahler's life as a perpetual outsider, as a Jew in the anti-Semitic Europe of his day, must have struck a sympathetic note in the musicians who had also experienced that alienation. The love-hate relationship with *fin-de-siècle* Vienna that pervades Mahler's music also spoke personally to the older generation of the orchestra. The First Symphony, quoting "Songs of a Wayfarer" and dotted with folk tunes from his native Bohemia, seemed to tell the story of an entire civilization, which had once also been their civilization.

Bernstein understood this, and somehow Mahler's tortured soul seemed to mirror his own. In his performances of the First Symphony with the IPO (and there were many), he conveyed every orchestral color, every melodic fragment, every instrumental flourish as perhaps only a fellow composer could. To the audience, Bernstein's gestures may have seemed large and sweeping, but for the players, each beat was absolutely clear and even subdivided, assuring precision, yet never at the expense of the longer musical line. There was not a part of his body that did not somehow move to the music, and often at different times in response to the counter-rhythms. Far from being merely a showman, Bernstein had developed a stick technique that was incredibly sophisticated and varied. Yet he never depended solely on that. His face was a guide to the subtleties of the music, and he seemed able to convey more with his eyes closed than most conductors could with their eyes open. This ability, combined with the empathy that both Bernstein and Mahler aroused in the orchestra, made for an electrifying interpretation.

There was, however, one magical moment that still stands out in my mind above all the rest. It occurred in the beginning of the third movement, after the initial theme of *"Frère Jacques"* in the minor mode had been played. The next few measures consist of a lazily dotted melody played by two oboes starting off a bit slowly (*ziemlich langsam*) and gradually building in speed and intensity. It is a theme of the utmost delicacy and nuance, and can easily be destroyed by too heavy-handed an approach. At that point, I looked up from the music in amazement to see that Bernstein had put down his baton and was swaying very slightly back and forth on the podium, his hands in the air, snapping his fingers to the music. The whole orchestra seemed to be dancing with him. It was like a scene out of the *Klezmers*, and it was totally authentic. I think that Mahler himself would have joined in, had he been present.

There will always be disagreements among musicians and music lovers alike concerning the most faithful rendering of a composer's intentions. Performers, including orchestras and conductors, play the role of facilitators, middlemen. The task begins with consideration of the metronome markings and dynamics, listening for proper balances among the instruments, and many other similar details. But it is also necessary to understand the environment in which the music was created, the prevailing values of the period and the kind of society in which the composer thrived or struggled. In the case of Mahler, Bernstein not only understood the composer, he was a soulmate. And the IPO provided the perfect vehicle for Bernstein to communicate his unique understanding. My experiences playing Mahler in the Israel Philharmonic Orchestra under Leonard Bernstein were an education: in music, in history, and in what might be called the human spirit. It was then that life and art seemed to meet.

A piano rehearsal with the recently-founded Tanglewood Festival Chorus, 1971

Beethoven in Excelsis

by JOHN OLIVER

WHEN the Tanglewood Festival Chorus was founded in January 1970, its purpose was to provide the Boston Symphony Orchestra with a resident choir for the summer season. Shortly after auditions were held, however, the management came to me and asked whether we would be willing to sing the Ninth Symphony of Beethoven with Leonard Bernstein in Symphony Hall on April 11, three months before our scheduled debut at Tanglewood. Could we! Not only would we start our new musical adventure in Symphony Hall itself, but Leonard Bernstein would lead our first concert. Life could not get more exciting than this.

Our first Tanglewood weekend opened with Seiji Ozawa conducting Composer Bernstein's *Chichester Psalms* and ended with Maestro Bernstein conducting the Mahler Second Symphony. I remember vividly the moment when Lenny came to the West Barn to have the piano rehearsal of the Mahler. He was flamboyant. He chain-smoked. He was kind and considerate to everyone (particularly to this young conductor, whose desire to create the most beautiful chorus ever heard was almost painfully palpable at the time.) Most of all he was tenacious. I had never before seen anyone repeat the same phrase over and over, each time uncovering a new layer of beauty, a new layer of meaning. He was tireless in his pursuit of his own inner vision, a vision that illuminated all of our lives in the most profound way. Rather than feeling defeated by this repetition or in some way criticized by it, we felt humbled by the music itself and drawn into

John Oliver has been director of the Tanglewood Festival Chorus since its inception. He is also director of choral activities at the Massachusetts Institute of Technology and of the vocal program at the Tanglewood Music Center.

it in the deepest and most unself-conscious way. This was to be the pattern of all our work with Lenny, and we always went away the richer for it.

Probably the most memorable experience we had with Lenny was with Beethoven's *Missa Solemnis* in our second Tanglewood season. We gathered in the cold and damp on the Shed stage at six o'clock on the evening of July 21, 1971. I warmed up the chorus and gave a few final notes in the usual way, and Maestro Bernstein joined us at seven. We worked and worked. At ten o'clock we had only begun to rehearse the Credo. Shortly before midnight the bass soloist, Sherrill Milnes, had had enough and left the stage after an extremely colorful exchange with Lenny. Still we worked, the remaining soloists bundled up in scarves borrowed from the management office.

Only when the hour was coursing towards 1:00 a.m. and after we had promised to reappear at eight in the morning were we released into the chilly night. The Credo was not yet finished. At 8:00 a.m. we were back at work. Lenny, looking fresh as a daisy, said, "You are mighty good to come at this hour . . . and so am I!" Three days later we had a performance of this great work of such power and beauty that it remains in my mind, whole and elusive, to this moment.

Our lives have been enriched and elevated for our having had the privilege of participating in Leonard Bernstein's music-making. We salute him and deeply thank him and wish him many more wonderful years.

Brahms: Breaking the Fetters

by JAMES ORLEANS

LEONARD BERNSTEIN was already conducting the New York Phil-harmonic when I was just five years old. I grew up in a small suburban New Jersey town west of Manhattan. My family was not a particularly musical one, and we did not follow the musical events of the day. But our television, my childhood window on the world, brought us the news, the culture, the glamor of New York City. My few early recollections of Leonard Bernstein, the celebrity, came pri-marily from television: a news clip here, part of a *Young People's Concert* broadcast there. I didn't understand much of what he said or did, but, even as a youngster, I felt a strong, energized personality behind the TV image.

It was much later that I became acquainted with Bernstein, the musician, through his recordings with the New York Philharmonic Orchestra. Some of my favorites were William Schuman's Third Symphony, Shostakovich's First and Fifth symphonies and Stravin-sky's *Le Sacre du Printemps*. What impressed me most about these performances was the way the conductor was able to sustain the sound of the orchestra, especially at extremely slow tempos. I was beginning to understand why this man was a celebrity and what it was that made him a great conductor. It wasn't long before I began to believe that Bernstein was the only conductor alive who really knew how to extract the innermost beauty from an Adagio.

My first personal encounter with Bernstein the teacher came much later, when I was a fellow in the Tanglewood Music Center Orchestra during the summer of 1981. I had just completed a degree program

James Orleans has been a member of the Boston Symphony Orchestra's double bass section since 1983.

at Boston Conservatory; a summer at Tanglewood, a daydream I had only fleetingly entertained a decade before, lay ahead. It held thrilling prospects for me. One of them was the opportunity to meet and perform under the baton of Leonard Bernstein.

The orchestra had been performing together for only a few weeks when Bernstein arrived. We were all on edge with anticipation. As he strode across the stage to the podium, it was his small physical stature and slight paunch that first struck me as incongruous with my expectations. But as he spoke and began to work, his persona filled the proscenium. He started the rehearsal having already reduced the strings for the Mozart symphony on the program. As we got further into the first movement, he appeared displeased with the balance. Apparently the bass section was still too large. He leveled his gaze at me. "I'm afraid I shall have to cut back the section by one more player." I was the last bassist and therefore the one to leave. Wanting very much to stay, I chanced a request. "Maestro," I pleaded, "I promise to play sensitively." He smiled generously, amused (to my relief) by the remark, and allowed me to remain. Later in the week there was a TMC barbecue in honor of the musical guests. Mr. Bernstein was present. I introduced myself, and much to my surprise, he recognized me instantly. "Oh, yes, the sensitive one," he exclaimed, and gave me the ubiquitous Bernstein embrace. I have not yet reintroduced myself to him since I joined the Boston Sympony Orchestra.

Experiencing Bernstein, the Maestro, from within the BSO is very different from the TMCO perspective. With the student orchestra, he appeared the consummate didact, eloquently digressing, continually using the piano to illustrate a point, and completely losing track of time. I remember his going to the piano in the middle of a rehearsal and re-harmonizing a melody from Hindemith's Concert Music for Strings and Brass, transforming it into a jaunty little cabaret tune. Although he still loses track of rehearsal time (more crucial when dealing with a professional orchestra), his work with the BSO is much more intense. I cannot think of a more demanding conductor than Leonard Bernstein. He will bellow in displeasure, castigating the musicians for lack of concentration or nonchalance, when something is not just right. But he utterly melts, praising the players to the heights, when something beautiful happens. It is obvious that he loves the orchestra and expects great things from it. Often, he gets just that.

Bernstein leading the Boston Symphony Orchestra in the
Symphony No. 1 of Johannes Brahms on the evening of July 20,
1985, following an exciting open rehearsal the same morning

The crowning lesson in my (now lifelong) "study" of Bernstein came during the Tanglewood summer of 1985. For his program he had chosen Brahms's First Piano Concerto and his First Symphony. It was the Saturday morning open dress rehearsal. The Shed was crowded, as it usually is when Bernstein conducts. The Maestro greeted the ovation and launched the orchestra into the absolutely greatest performance it has achieved in the five years I have been a member.

From the opening C-minor chords of this symphony, I felt it was destined to be a momentous event. The involvement onstage was total. I felt the energy from every member of the orchestra. I remember distinctly the B-major chord of the first movement's second ending appearing to me for the first time as emanating from a great pipe organ, the sonority of the orchestra was so astonishingly rich. The finale was even more remarkable. I recall how powerful the opening of the Adagio was; how slowly but inexorably those three quarter-notes in the bass line, along with the roll of the timpani, built toward the first portentous downbeat of the movement; how satisfyingly the energy from that passionate outburst was relaxed over the next four measures. Bernstein held onto the moment like a poignant memory one reluctantly allows to recede. His masterful control of the Adagio gave it a depth that I had not perceived ever before. The woodwind solos were magnificent. One listener described Doriot Dwyer's flute solo as an incredible beacon of sound that filled the Shed.

Not a soul in the orchestra was left untouched by the experience. They had all been moved to involve themselves completely, to spend themselves fully in service to the music and Bernstein's vision of it. I noticed much head-shaking amongst the players backstage in utter amazement at the miracle that had just happened. How we were going to do it again in the evening was an unspoken question.

For me the experience was truly a musical revelation. It made me realize that my understanding of the great music of the past had been colored by the teaching and performance practice of the day, that my attendance to historical and stylistic concerns had blinded me to the true essence of much of the music I performed as an orchestra musician, and that routine performances of these works do nothing but reinforce and perpetuate such categorical thinking. Bernstein's visionary performance of Brahms's First Symphony revealed to me the emotional core of the work. The music then broke free of its historical and stylistic fetters and became a vital, living entity.

That evening was the actual public concert. The capacity audience was treated to a magnificent performance; but I shall always remember the extraordinary dress rehearsal. It could not have been repeated. I have often wondered since then if it could happen like that for me ever again. However, my hopes always run their highest when Leonard Bernstein approaches the podium in the Shed at Tanglewood.

Appendices

A Leonard Bernstein Calendar

THIS summary of the principal events in Bernstein's career has been adapted with the editor's permission from the fuller listing in *Leonard Bernstein: A Complete Catalogue of His Work*, ed. Jack Gottlieb (New York: Jalni Publications, Inc., 1988).

Abbreviations:
BSO = Boston Symphony Orchestra
IPO = Israel Philharmonic Orchestra
LB = Leonard Bernstein
NSO = National Symphony Orchestra
NYC = New York City
NYP = New York Philharmonic
VSO = Vienna State Opera

Year	Age	
1918		Born August 25, Lawrence, Mass.
1928	10	First piano lessons, with Frieda Karp.
1930	11	Graduated W. L. Garrison Grammar School, Roxbury, Mass.
1931	13	Became Bar Mitzvah, Temple Mishkan Tefila, Boston, Mass.
		Piano lessons with Susan Williams at New England Conservatory of Music.
1932	14	Piano lessons with Heinrich Gebhard and his assistant, Helen Coates.
1935	16	Graduated Boston Latin School.
	17	Piano study continued with Gebhard.
1938	19	June 12, first known public appearance as composer-pianist: *Music for the Dance*, Nos. 1 & 2, *Music for Two Pianos*.

Year	Age	
1939	20	April 21, first appearance as conductor, leading his own incidental score to *The Birds*, at Harvard University.
		June 22, graduated Harvard, cum laude.
		Summer, conducted Boston Pops on Esplanade (Brahms: *Academic Festival Overture*, performed without rehearsal).
	21	Entered Curtis Institute of Music, Philadelphia.
1940		Spent first summer as student of Serge Koussevitzky at Tanglewood.
1941	22	May 3, received diploma from Curtis Institute.
1942	23	April 21, premiere of Sonata for Clarinet and Piano, Boston, David Glazer and Leonard Bernstein.
		Summer, named assistant to Koussevitzky at Tanglewood.
1942–43	24	Worked at Harms, Inc., New York publishers, using pseudonym of Lenny Amber.
1943		August 24, premiere of *I Hate Music*, LB and Jennie Tourel, Lenox, MA.
	25	August 25, invited to be assistant conductor of the Philharmonic-Society of New York by Artur Rodzinski.
		November 14, made debut with NYP, substituting for conductor Bruno Walter.
		December 16, substituted for conductor Howard Barlow at NYP.
1944		January 28, premiere of *Jeremiah*, Symphony No. 1, Pittsburgh Symphony Orchestra, LB conducting, with Jennie Tourel.
		March 4, conducted first concert outside of US: Les Symphoniques de Montreal.
		April 18, conducted premiere of *Fancy Free*, NYC.
	26	December 28, premiere of *On the Town*, NYC, Max Goberman, conductor.
1945		January 14, led first performance of *Fancy Free Suite*, Pittsburgh.
		May 11, premiere of *Hashkivenu*, Park Avenue Synagogue, NYC, Max Helfman, conductor.
	27	October 8, began three-year directorship of the New York City Symphony.
1946		May 15, led first performance overseas, Czech Philharmonic, Prague.

Year	Age	
1946		July 4, conducted European premiere of *Fancy Free* with Ballet Theater at Covent Garden, London.
		August 6, conducted American premiere of Britten's *Peter Grimes*, Tanglewood.
	28	October 24, led premiere of *Facsimile*, Ballet Theater, NYC.
1947		April 27, gave first of nine concerts with Palestine Symphony Orchestra, Tel Aviv.
1948	30	October 2–28, led concerts of IPO during the War of Independence.
1949		April 8, premiere of *The Age of Anxiety*, Symphony No. 2, BSO, Koussevitzky conducting, LB as soloist.
1950	31	April 24, premiere of *Peter Pan*, NYC, Ben Steinberg, cond.
1951	32	Became head of orchestra and conducting departments of Berkshire Music Center (Tanglewood) (annually through 1955, but not 1954).
	33	September 9, married Chilean actress and pianist, Felicia Montealegre Cohn.
		Became professor of music at Brandeis University (through 1954).
1952		June 12, led premiere of *Trouble in Tahiti*, Brandeis University.
	34	September 8, daughter born: Jamie Anne Maria.
1953		February 26, premiere of *Wonderful Town*, NYC, Lehman Engel, cond.
	35	December, became first American to conduct at La Scala, Milan: Cherubini's *Medea* with Maria Callas.
1954		July 28, *On the Waterfront* released by Columbia Pictures.
	36	September 12, premiere of *Serenade*, Isaac Stern, LB, and IPO, Venice.
		November 14, wrote and performed his first *Omnibus* telecast, on the sketches of Beethoven's Fifth Symphony.
1955		February 23, European premiere of *Wonderful Town*, Princes Theatre, London
		July 7, son born: Alexander Serge Leonard.
		August 11, led premiere of *Suite from On the Waterfront*, Tanglewood.
	37	October 28, premiere of *The Lark*, Boston; November 17, opening in NYC.

Year	Age	
1956		March, European premiere of *Trouble in Tahiti*, performed in German at the Cologne Opera, Germany.
		April 2, signed first contract with CBS.
	38	October 15, named one of two principal conductors (the other being Dimitri Mitropoulos) of the NYP, the first American-born and -trained conductor to be so designated.
		November 9, first performance in German of *Wonderful Town* at the Volksoper in Vienna.
		December 1, premiere of *Candide*, NYC, Samuel Krachmalnik, cond.
1957		January 2, directed first concert as co-conductor of NYP.
		January 26, led premiere of *Overture to Candide* (concert version), NYP.
	39	September 26, premiere of *West Side Story*, Max Goberman, cond.
		November 19, named music director of NYP.
1958		January 18, began first series of televised NYP *Young People's Concerts* on CBS-TV, beginning with "What Does Music Mean?"
	40	Oct 3, commenced eleven-year period as music director of NYP.
1959		February 20, Amberson Enterprises, Inc., founded with Helen Coates, Abraham Freedman, and H. Gordon Freeman as directors.
	41	August–September, NYP tour of seventeen European and Near East countries, including two weeks in the USSR.
		November, publication of first book, *The Joy of Music*, Simon & Schuster, publisher.
1960		January, led concerts for Mahler centennial, NYP.
1961	42	January 19, premiered his *Fanfare* at Inaugural Gala for John F. Kennedy, Washington, D.C.
		February 9, first foreign production of *West Side Story*, Sidney, Australia.
		February 13, all-Bernstein program, NYP, including premiere of *Symphonic Dances from West Side Story*, Lukas Foss, cond.
1962	43	February 28, daughter born: Nina Maria Felicia.
	44	September 23, led inaugural concert of NYP in Philharmonic Hall, Lincoln Center, NYC.

Year	Age	
1962		Autumn, publication of his second book, *Leonard Bernstein's Young People's Concerts for Reading and Listening*, Simon & Schuster.
1963		May 30, London premiere of *On the Town*, Prince of Wales Theatre.
	45	November 24, led JFK memorial televised concert with NYP.
		December 10, led premiere of *Kaddish*, Symphony No. 3, IPO, Tel Aviv, with Hannah Rovina, Jennie Tourel, et al.
1964		March 6, debut at Metropolitan Opera, conducting Verdi's *Falstaff*.
1965	46	July 15, led premiere of his *Chichester Psalms*, NYP.
1966	47	March 14, debut at VSO with Verdi's *Falstaff*.
	48	November, publication of his third book, *The Infinite Variety of Music*, Simon & Schuster.
1967		July 9, conducted IPO on Mt. Scopus, after the "Six Day War."
1968	49	February 28, first performance in German of *West Side Story, Volksoper*, Vienna.
		April 13, led first of five performances of Strauss's *Der Rosenkavalier* at the VSO.
		June 8, conducted members of the NYP at Robert Kennedy's funeral, St. Patrick's Cathedral, NYC.
1969	50	May 17, last concert as music director of NYP, after having conducted 939 concerts with the orchestra, more than anyone else in its history. Gave 36 world premieres, 14 United States premieres, 15 New York City premieres, and more than 40 works not previously performed by the NYP. Received title of "Laureate Conductor."
1970	51	July, became advisor to Tanglewood through 1974 with Seiji Ozawa and Gunther Schuller as artistic directors.
1971	52	January 19, signed first contract with Unitel for the filming of Mahler and Brahms symphonies.
	53	September 8, John F. Kennedy Center for the Performing Arts, Washington, D.C., opened with premiere of *Mass*, Maurice Peress, cond./Gordon Davidson, dir.
		December 15, conducted his 1000th concert with the NYP, a milestone unequaled in the orchestra's history.
1972		March 28, premiere of *Meditations I & II* for cello and piano, NYC, LB and Stephen Kates.

Year	Age	
1972	54	September, signed first contract with DG (Polygram Records) to record *Carmen*.
1973		January 19, led Concert for Peace at National Cathedral, Washington, with NSO.
		June 23, gave concert with RAI (Rome) Orchestra and choruses, at the Vatican, Rome, for the tenth anniversary of Paul VI's elevation to the Papacy.
		June 25, European premiere of *Mass, Konzerthaus*, Vienna, Yale Symphony Orchestra, John Mauceri, cond.
	55	October 9, delivered first of six lectures entitled *The Unanswered Question*, as the Charles Eliot Norton Professor of Poetry at Harvard University.
1974		May 16, led premiere of *The Dybbuk*, NYC Ballet, choreography by Jerome Robbins.
		July, conducted BSO at Tanglewood, commemorating Koussevitzky's centennial.
	56	August 16, led world premiere of *Dybbuk Variations* in Auckland, New Zealand.
1975	57	April 3 and 17, American premieres of *Dybbuk Suites*, Nos. 1 and 2, respectively (new titles for *Dybbuk Variations*), NYP.
1976		February, his fourth book published, *The Unanswered Question*, Harvard University Press.
		May 8, premiere of *1600 Pennsylvania Avenue*, NYC, Roland Gagnon, cond.
		August 5, European premiere of *Candide*, in German, Wiener Stadthalle, Vienna.
	58	October 8, benefit concert for Jimmy Carter's campaign, Washingon, D.C.
1977		January 19, conducted at Inaugural Concert for President Jimmy Carter, Kennedy Center, Washington, D.C.
		March-April, IPO presented a two-week nationwide festival of LB's music to celebrate the 30th anniversary of his first concerts with the orchestra.
	59	October 11, premiere of *Slava!*, led by Mstislav Rostropovich, and premieres of *Three Meditations from Mass* and *Songfest*, LB cond., NSO.
1978		January 29, conducted *Fidelio*, first live telecast (to 18 countries) from VSO.
		June 16, death of Felicia Montealegre Bernstein.

Year	Age	
1978		July 22, European premiere of *Three Meditations from Mass* at the Carinthian Summer Festival, Villach, Austria.
	60	August 25, Leonard Bernstein 60th Birthday Celebration Concert, NSO, Wolf Trap, Virginia.
		November 22, led European premiere of *Songfest* in Munich with the Bavarian Radio Symphony Orchestra.
1979	61	December 22, premieres of two ballets to *Songfest* and *The Age of Anxiety*, John Neumeier, choreographer, Klauspeter Seibel, cond., Hamburg, Germany.
1980		January 17, premiere of newly choreographed version of *Dybbuk: Suite of Dances* (from the *Dybbuk Variations*), NYC Ballet, Jerome Robbins, choreographer, Robert Irving, conductor.
	62	September 25, premiere of *Divertimento*, BSO, Seiji Ozawa, cond.
		October 11, premiere of *A Musical Toast*, NYP, Zubin Mehta, cond.
		November 14, conducted *Lincoln Portrait*, with Copland as narrator, on Copland's 80th birthday (NSO, Washington, D.C.).
		December 7, received Kennedy Center Honors for Lifetime of Contributions to American Culture through the Performing Arts, Washington, D.C.
1981		February 16, first performance of *Mass* in German, at VSO, Maurice Peress, cond.
		May 27, led premiere of *Ḥalil*, with Jean-Pierre Rampal, IPO, Tel Aviv.
1982	63	January–February, fellow-in-residence at Indiana University. Directed workshops with Stephen Wadsworth on their new opera *A Quiet Place*.
		July–August, as artistic director of Los Angeles Philharmonic Institute, gave master classes in conducting.
	64	Opera-house version of *Candide* opened at NYC Opera, Lincoln Center, John Mauceri, cond.
1983		June 17, premiere of *A Quiet Place* (first version), Houston Grand Opera, John DeMain, cond.
	65	August 25, Leonard Bernstein Day, Lawrence, Mass., dedicated to nuclear disarmament: parade, concert, dedication of LB Outdoor Theater in Heritage State Park.
		December 3, pianist at Artur Rubinstein memorial concert at Carnegie Hall, NYC.

Year	Age	

1983   December 31, first New Year's Eve appearance at Cathedral of St. John the Divine, NYC, speaking on anti-nuclear and peace causes.

1984   June 19, premiere of revised version of *A Quiet Place* at La Scala, Milan, John Mauceri, cond.

July 22, opening of *A Quiet Place* at Kennedy Center Opera House, Washington, D.C., John Mauceri, cond.

66   December 2, wedding of daughter, Jamie, to David Evan Thomas.

1985   July–August, with European Community Orchestra, toured in a "Journey for Peace" program (including *Kaddish*) to Athens, Hiroshima (commemoration of 40th anniversary of atomic bomb), Budapest, Vienna, sharing conducting with Eiji Oue.

67   September 26, opening of *Bernstein: The Television Work* at the Museum of Broadcasting, NYC.

1986   April 10, led *A Quiet Place* with Austrian Radio Symphony Orchestra at the VSO, recorded by DG.

68   September 12, led premiere of *Jubilee Games* with IPO, Avery Fisher Hall, NYC.

December 15, led premiere of *Opening Prayer*, NYP, Carnegie Hall.

1987   March 4, granddaughter Francisca Ann Maria born to Jamie and David Thomas.

March 8, premiere of *A Quiet Place* in German, Bielefeld, Germany, Rainer Koch, cond.

April–May, workshop on musical adaptation (not completed) of Brecht play by LB, Jerome Robbins, John Guare, and Stephen Sondheim: *The Race to Urga* at Mitzi Newhouse Theater, Lincoln Center, NYC.

1988   69   May 9, premiere of *Arias and Barcarolles*, Joyce Castle, Louise Edeiken, John Brandstetter, Mordechi Kaston, singers, LB and Michael Tilson Thomas, pianists, Equitable Center Auditorium, NYC.

May 11, sang premiere of his song *My Twelve-Tone Melody* in honor of Irving Berlin's 100th birthday, Carnegie Hall, NYC.

May 21, premiere of expanded opera house version of *Candide*, Glasgow, John Mauceri, cond.

70   August 25–28, LB 70th Birthday Celebration, Tanglewood.

The Music of Leonard Bernstein

A CHRONOLOGICAL LIST

THIS list of Bernstein's compositions is arranged by the year of composition; some works were subsequently revised. Frequently a title serves for more than one form of a piece (e.g., *On the Town*, which is the title of a musical comedy and of a set of "Three Dance Episodes" for orchestra). Alternate versions are here indicated after the original title. Full information is contained in *Leonard Bernstein: A Complete Catalogue of His Work*, ed. Jack Gottlieb (New York: Jalni Publications, Inc., 1988), from which this brief listing has been drawn, with the editor's permission. The same publication also provides a complete listing of Bernstein's published books and articles. His television programs to 1985 are listed (with dates of broadcast and summaries of the contents) in *Leonard Bernstein: The Television Work*, a catalogue with photographs and interpretive articles published by the Museum of Broadcasting, New York, in conjunction with an exhibition of Bernstein's television work in fall 1985.

Year	Title
1937	**Piano Trio**
1938	**Piano Sonata**
1940	**Sonata for Violin and Piano**
1942	**Sonata for Clarinet and Piano**
	Jeremiah, Symphony No. 1
1943	**Seven Anniversaries,** for piano
	I Hate Music, A Cycle of Five Kid Songs for Soprano and Piano
1944	**Fancy Free:** Ballet, Suite [withdrawn], and Three Dance Variations
	On the Town: Musical Comedy and Three Dance Episodes
1945	**Hashkivenu,** for Cantorial Solo, SATB Choir, and Organ
	Afterthought, for Voice and Piano [withdrawn]

Year   Title

1946   **Facsimile:** Ballet and Choreographic Essay

1947   **La Bonne Cuisine,** Four Recipes for Voice and Piano
        Simchu Na, for Chorus and Orchestra or Piano
        Reena, for Chorus and Orchestra

1948   **Brass Music,** Five Pieces for Four Brass Players and Piano
        Four Anniversaries, for Piano

1949   **Two Love Songs,** on Poems of Rilke, for Voice and Piano
        The Age of Anxiety, Symphony No. 2 for Piano and Orchestra
        Prelude, Fugue, and Riffs, for Solo Clarinet and Jazz Ensemble

1950   **Peter Pan,** Songs and Choruses for the Play
        Yigdal, Round for Chorus and Piano

1951   **Five Anniversaries,** for Piano
        Silhouette (Galilee), Song for Voice and Piano
        Trouble in Tahiti, Opera in One Act

1953   **Wonderful Town,** Musical Comedy

1954   **Serenade (after Plato's "Symposium"),** for Solo Violin, String Orchestra, Harp, and Percussion
        On the Waterfront, Film Score and Suite (1955)

1955   **The Lark,** French and Latin Choruses
        Get Hep!, Marching Song
        Salome, Incidental Music [withdrawn]

1956   **Candide,** Comic Operetta and Overture

1957   **Two Harvard Choruses,** Male Chorus and Piano [withdrawn]
        West Side Story, Musical

1958   **The Firstborn,** Incidental Music [withdrawn]

1960   **Symphonic Dances from *West Side Story*,** for Orchestra

1961   **Two Fanfares,** for Orchestral Ensembles

1963   **Kaddish,** Symphony No. 3 for Orchestra, Mixed Chorus, Boys' Choir, Speaker, and Soprano Solo

1965   **Chichester Psalms,** for Mixed Choir, Boy Soloist, and Orchestra
        Two Anniversaries, for piano

1968   **So Pretty,** Song for Voice and Piano

1969   **Shivaree,** for Double Brass Ensemble and Percussion

1970   **Warm-Up,** Round for Mixed Chorus

1971   **Mass,** A Theatre Piece for Singers, Players, and Dancers
        Two Meditations from *Mass*, for Orchestra

Year	Title
1972	Two Meditations from *Mass*, for Violoncello and Piano
1973	'if you can't eat you got to', for Male Chorus
1974	The Dybbuk, Ballet and Suites
	Songs Without Words, for piano
1975	By Bernstein, A Musical Cabaret [based on deleted materials from previous theater works] [withdrawn]
1976	1600 Pennsylvania Avenue, A Musical about the Problems of Housekeeping
1977	Three Meditations from *Mass*, for Violoncello and Orchestra
	Three Meditations from *Mass*, for Violoncello and Piano
	Songfest, A Cycle of American Poems for Six Singers and Orchestra
	Slava!, Overture for Orchestra/Band
	CBS Music, for Orchestra [withdrawn]
1979	Up! Up! Up! and My New Friends, Songs for Voice and Piano
	Piccola Serenata, for Voice and Piano
1980	Divertimento, for Orchestra/Band
	A Musical Toast, for Orchestra/Band
	Touches, for Piano
1981	Ḥalil, Nocturne for Solo Flute and Small Orchestra
	Moby Diptych, for Piano
	Olympic Hymn, for Mixed Choir and Orchestra [withdrawn]
1983	A Quiet Place, Opera in Three Acts
1986	Jubilee Games, for Orchestra
	Sean Song, for Voice and Strings
	Opening Prayer, for Orchestra with Baritone Solo
1987	Trial Song, from *The Race to Urga*
1988	Missa Brevis, for A Cappella Chorus with Incidental Percussion
	My Twelve-Tone Melody, Song for Voice and Piano
	Thirteen Anniversaries, for Piano
	Arias and Barcarolles, for Piano Four-Hands and Mixed Voices

A Discography of the Composer

by J. F. WEBER

All recordings are 33 rpm long-play records, with the exception of those identified as "78" or "45" (the number representing the rpm) or "CD" (compact disc).

Abbreviations:

bar	= baritone	perc	= percussion
cl	= clarinet	rec.	= recorded
ct	= countertenor	sop	= soprano
fl	= flute	ten	= tenor
f.p.	= first performance	tpt	= trumpet
hp	= harp	trb	= trombone
m-s	= mezzo-soprano	treb	= treble
org	= organ	vln	= violin

Sonata for Clarinet and Piano (1941 – 42; f.p. April 21, 1942)

David Oppenheim, cl, Leonard Bernstein, pf, Hargail set MW 501 (78) — 1944

Herbert Tichman, cl, Ruth Budnevich, pf, Concert Hall H-18 — 1954

William Willett, cl, James Staples, pf, Mark MRS 32638 — 1970

Stanley Druckner, cl, Leonid Hambro, pf, Odyssey Y-30942 — rec. April 1970

Jack Snavely, cl, Jeffrey Hollander, pf, Golden Crest RE-7035 — 1972

J. F. Weber is a Catholic priest who works in hospitals in Utica, N.Y. As a discographer, his work appears regularly in *Fanfare* Magazine. He also publishes his own series of discographies, and he describes a forthcoming volume on Gregorian chant recordings as his "magnum opus."

Jerome Bunke, cl, Hidemitsu Hayashi, pf, Musical Heritage Society MHS 1887 — 1974

John Russo, cl, Lydia W. Ignacio, pf, Orion ORS 79330 — 1980

Lynn Holman, cl, G. Humphrey, pf, Bedivere BVR 311 — 1985

Joaquin Valdepeñas, cl, Patricia Parr, pf, Musica Viva MVCD 1016 (CD) — 1987

Jeremiah, Symphony No. 1 (1941 – 44; f.p. Jan. 28, 1944)

Nan Merriman, m-s, St. Louis Symphony Orch — Leonard Bernstein, RCA Victor 11-8971-3 in set DM 1026 (78); Camden CAL 196; R.C.A. SMA 7002 — rec. Dec. 1, 1945

Jennie Tourel, m-s, New York Philharmonic — Leonard Bernstein, Columbia ML 5703; MS 6303; set MG 72793; C.B.S. 72399; set 78228; 75DC 390-92 (CD — Japan) — rec. May 20, 1961

Christa Ludwig, m-s, Israel Philharmonic Orch — Leonard Bernstein, D.G. 2530968; set 2709077; 415964 (CD) — rec. August 1977

Seven Anniversaries, for piano (1942 – 43)

Leonard Bernstein, pf, Hargail set MW 501 (78) — 1944 (N.B. 2, 5, 7 only)

Leonard Bernstein, pf, RCA Victor 12-0683 in set DM 1278 (78); Camden CAL 214; R.C.A. SMA 7015 — rec. Sept. 17, 1947 (N.B. 1, 2, 3 only)

Leonard Bernstein, pf, RCA Victor 12-0228 in set DM 1209 (78); 18-0114 in set DV 15 (78); Camden CAL 214; CAL 351; R.C.A. SMA 7015 — rec. Sept. 17, 1947 (N.B. 4, 5 only)

Leonard Bernstein, pf, Camden CAL 214; CAL 351; R.C.A. SMA 7015 — rec. Sept. 17, 1947 (N.B. 6, 7 only)

James Tocco, pf, Pro Arte PAD/CDD 109 (CD); 18038 — rec. March 23 – 27, 1982

I Hate Music — song cycle (1943; f.p. August 24, 1943)

Barbra Streisand, Columbia CS 9136 — 1965 (My name is Barbara only)

Roberta Alexander, sop, Tan Crone, pf, Etcetera ETC/KTC 1037 (CD); MHS 7450 — 1985

Fancy Free — ballet (1944; f.p. April 18, 1944)

Ballet Theater Orch — Leonard Bernstein, Decca 23463-6 in set DA 406 (78); DL 6023; Varese Sarabande VC 81055 — rec. 1944: the first side, "Big Stuff," sung by Billie Holliday with unidentified orchestra and conductor, was made at a separate recording session.

Ballet Theater Orch — Joseph Levine, Capitol P 8196; L 8197; set HDR 21004; CCL 7517 — rec. October 13, 1952

(*Continued*)

Columbia Symphony Orch — Leonard Bernstein, Columbia CL 920 — rec. July 13, 1956

New York Philharmonic — Leonard Bernstein, Columbia ML 6077; MS 6677; M 30304; set MG 32174; C.B.S. 72406; 30043; 61816; MLK 39448 (CD); 75DC 390-92 (CD — Japan) — rec. June 11, 1963 : three dances issued as ML 6271; MS 6871

Concert Arts Orch — Robert Irving, Time-Life Records STL 145; Capitol SP 870l; Seraphim S 60197; Columbia TWO 302 — rec. 1966

Israel Philharmonic Orch — Leonard Bernstein, D.G. 2531196 — rec. 1978

St. Louis Symphony Orch — Leonard Slatkin, Angel DS-37358; CDC 47522 (CD); EL 270510 — rec. October 1985

———— three dances

Boston Pops Orch — Arthur Fiedler, RCA Victor 11-9386 (78) — rec. June 5, 1946

Philadelphia Orch Pops — Alexander Hilsberg, Columbia AAL 17 — rec. Jan. 3, l952

Boston Pops Orch — Arthur Fiedler, RCA Victor LM 1726; WDM 1726 (45); ERA 146 (45) — rec. June 25, 1952

Boston Pops Orch — Arthur Fiedler, RCA Victor LM/LSC 2294; LM/LSC 2747; ARL 1-0108 — rec. June 18, 1958

Cleveland Pops Orch — Louis Lane, Epic LC 3626; BC 1047; Columbia SX 1583; SCX 3503 — rec. July 22-23, 1959 (danzon only)

Royal Philharmonic Orch — Eric Rogers, London SPC 21048; Decca PFS 4211 — 1971 (finale, opening dance, coda only)

On the Town — musical (1944; f.p. in New York Dec. 28, 1944)

Nancy Walker, orch — Leonard Joy, Decca 23396 in set A 416 (78) — rec. Feb. 1, 1945 (Ya got me; I can cook too)

Mary Martin, orch — Tutti Camerata, Decca 23395 in set A 416 (78) — rec. Feb. 6, 1945 (Lucky to be me; Lonely town)

Lyn Murray Chorus and Orch — Lyn Murray, Decca 23485 in set A 416 (78) — rec. Sept. 14, 1945 (Opening, New York, New York)

Betty Comden, Adolph Green, orch — Lyn Murray, Decca 23485 in set A 416 (78) — rec. Sept. 14, 1945 (I get carried away)

(all six numbers above) Decca DL 8030; Ace of Hearts AH 129

Nancy Walker, Betty Comden, Adolph Green, Cris Alexander (in their original roles), John Reardon, George Gaynes, Randel Striboneen, chorus and orch — Leonard Bernstein, Columbia OL 5540; OS 2028; S 31005; Philips BBL 7462; SBBL 613; 847089 — rec. May 31, 1960

(Continued)

Lionel Blair, Noele Gordon, Dennis Lotis, Shane Rimmer, Stella Tanner, Williams Singers, orch — Geoff Love, Columbia SCX 3281 — 1960

Carol Arthur, Don McKay, Elliott Gould, Gillian Lewis, chorus and orch. of the London production — Lawrence Leonard, C.B.S. APG/SAPG 60005 — rec. 1963

——— **overture**

orch — Lehman Engel, Columbia CL 1279; CS 8094 — 1959

——— **four dances** (three plus dream sequence)

On the Town Orch — Leonard Bernstein, RCA Victor 10-1158-62 in set M 995 (78); 10-1162-5 in set DM 995 (78); Camden CAL 196; CAL 336; CAE 203 (45) — rec. Feb. 3, 1945

——— **three dances**

Cleveland Pops Orch — Louis Lane, Epic LC 3743; BC 1107; Columbia SX/SCX 6048 — rec. July 7, l960

New York Philharmonic — Leonard Bernstein, Columbia ML 6077; MS 6677; M 30304; set MG 32174; C.B.S. 72406; 30043; 61816; MK 42263 (CD); MLK 39448 (CD) — rec. June 11, 1963

Royal Philharmonic Orch — Eric Rogers, London SPC 21048; Decca PFS 4211; 414382 — 1971 (Times Square only)

Israel Philharmonic Orch — Leonard Bernstein, D.G. 2532052; 415966 (CD) — rec. May 21 – 29, 1981

Boston Pops Orch — John Williams, Philips 416360 (CD) — rec. June 1985

St. Louis Symphony Orch — Leonard Slatkin, Angel DS-37358; CDC 47522 (CD); EL 270510 — 1986

Facsimile (1946; ballet f.p. October 24, 1946; choreographic essay f.p. March 5, 1947)

——— **ballet**

Ballet Theater Orch — Joseph Levine, Capitol P 8320; set HDR 21004 — rec. April 25, 1955

——— **choreographic essay**

RCA Victor Symphony Orch — Leonard Bernstein, RCA Victor 11-9677-8 in set DM 1142 (78); Camden CAL 196; R.C.A. SMA 7002 — rec. Jan. 24, 1947

New York Philharmonic — Leonard Bernstein, Columbia ML 6192; MS 6792; set MG 32174; C.B.S. 72374 — rec. June 18, 1963

(*Continued*)

Concert Arts Orch — Robert Irving, Time-Life Records SLT 159; Capitol SP 8701; Seraphim S 60197 — rec. 1967

Israel Philharmonic Orch — Leonard Bernstein, D.G. 2532052 — rec. May 21 – 29, 1981

St. Louis Symphony Orch — Leonard Slatkin, Angel DS-37358; CDC 47522 (CD); 270510 — 1986

La Bonne Cuisine (1947)

Felicia Sanders, orch — Irving Joseph, Decca DL 8762/78762 — 1958 (Rabbit at top speed only)

Roberta Alexander, sop, Tan Crone, pf, Etcetera ETC/KTC 1037 (CD); MHS 7450 — 1985 (N.B. sung twice, French and English)

Reena, Hebrew folk song transcription, arr. for chorus and orchestra (1947)

chorus and orch — Max Goberman, Vox 16040 in set VX 123 (78) — 1947

Simchu na; Hebrew song by Mattiyahu Weiner, arr. for chorus and piano (1947)

chorus and orch — Victor Young, Alco set A 21 (78); Alco 1009 — 1947

Brass Music (1947 – 48)

Joseph Eger, hr, Yaltah Menuhin, pf, RCA Victor LM 2146 — rec. 1956 (Elegy for Mippy I only)

Alan Raph, trb, Coronet S 1407 — 1969 (Elegy for Mippy II only)

Robert Gillespie, trb, Mace MCS 9112 — 1973 (Elegy for Mippy II only)

Cambridge Brass Quintet, Crystal S 204 — 1976 (Fanfare for Bima only)

Ronald-Kroeger Borror, trb, Crystal S-388 — 1983 (Elegy for Mippy II only)

Christian Lindberg, trb, BIS 318 (CD) — 1986 (Elegy for Mippy II only)

Thomas Stevens, tpt, Zito Carno, pf, Crystal S-665 — 1987 (Rondo for Lifey only)

Four Anniversaries (1948); **Five Anniversaries** (1949-51)

David Arden, pf, Musica Magna MM 50017 — 1977

James Tocco, pf, Pro Arte PAD/CDD 109 (CD); 18038 — rec. March 23 – 27, 1982

Leo Smit, pf, Musical Heritage Society MHS 7534; 60105 (CD) — 1986 (For Lukas Foss only)

The Age of Anxiety, Symphony No. 2 for Piano and Orchestra (1947 – 49/1965; f.p. April 8, 1949)

Lukas Foss, pf, New York PSO — Leonard Bernstein, Columbia MM 946 (78); ML 4325 — rec. Feb. 27, 1950 (original version)

Philippe Entremont, pf, New York Philharmonic — Leonard Bernstein, Columbia ML 6285; MS 6885; set MG 32793; C.B.S. 72503; set 78228; 75DC 390-92 (CD — Japan) — rec. July 19, 1965

Lukas Foss, pf, Israel Philharmonic Orch — Leonard Bernstein, D.G. 2530969; set 2709077; 415964 (CD) — rec. August 1977

Valeri Kamyshov, pf, Novosibirsk Philharmonic Orch — Arnold Kats, Melodiya S10-21411 — 1984

Prelude, Fugue, and Riffs (1949)

Benny Goodman, cl, Columbia Jazz Combo — Leonard Bernstein, Colum bia ML 6077; MS 6677; ML 6205; MS 6805; C.B.S. 72406; 72469; 61816; 39768; MK 42227 (CD); 75DC 390-92 (CD — Japan) — rec. Feb. 20 and May 6, 1963

Michael Collins, cl, London Sinfonietta — Simon Rattle, EMI 747991 (CD) — 1988

Peter Pan — songs for the Barrie play (1950; f.p. in New York April 24, 1950)

(*a*) Who am I; (Build) my house   (*c*) The pirate song; The plank
(*b*) Peter, Peter   (*d*) Never-never-land

Marcia Henderson (a,b), Boris Karloff and chorus (c), orch — Ben Steinberg, Columbia set MM 931 (78); ML 4312 — rec. June 1950

Evelyn Lear (a), sop, Martin Katz, pf, Mercury SRI 75136 — 1980

Roberta Alexander (a,d), sop, Tan Crone, pf, Etcetera ETC/KTC 1037 (CD); MHS 7450 — 1985

Two Love Songs (1949); **Silhouette** (1951)

Roberta Alexander, sop, Tan Crone, pf, Etcetera ETC/KTC 1037 (CD); MHS 7450 — 1985

Trouble in Tahiti — opera (1951; f.p. June 12, 1952)

CAST	SET A	SET B
Dinah	Beverly Wolff	Nancy Williams
Sam	David Atkinson	Julian Patrick
trio	Miriam Workman	Antonia Butler
	Earl Rogers	Michael Clarke
	Robert Bollinger	Mark Brown

(set A) MGM Orch — Arthur Winograd, M.G.M. E 3646; Heliodor H/HS 25020 (true stereo); Polydor 827845 (mono CD) — 1958

(*Continued*)

(set B) Columbia wind ensemble — Leonard Bernstein, Columbia KM/KMQ 32597 (quad) — rec. August 11, 13 – 15, 1973

(set C) included in A Quiet Place (below)

Wonderful Town — musical (1953; f.p. in New York Feb. 26, 1953)

CAST	SET A	SET B
Ruth	Rosalind Russell	Rosalind Russell
Eileen	Edith Adams	Jacquelyn McKeever
Robert Baker	George Gaynes	Sydney Chaplin
Chick Clark	Dort Clark	Sam Kirkham
Wreck	Jordan Bentley	Jordan Bentley
Frank Lippencott	Cris Alexander	Cris Alexander

(set A) chorus and orch. of the original production — Lehman Engel, Decca set DA 937 (78); Brunswick OE 9100-3 (78); set D 9-391 (45); DL 9010; DL 79010 (rechanneled); MCA 2050; Brunswick LAT 8058 — rec. March 8-9, 1953

Pat Kirkwood, Shani Wallis, Dennis Bowen, others, chorus, orch. of the London production, Columbia SEG 7569 (45); DB 3568-70 (78) — 1955 (highlights)

(set B) chorus and orch. of TV production — Lehmann Engel, Columbia OL 5360; OS 2008; Philips BBL 7307 — rec. Nov. 16, 1958

——— overture

orch — Lehman Engel, Columbia CL 1279; CS 8094 — 1959

Serenade for Violin, Strings and Percussion after Plato's Symposium (1954; f.p. Sept. 12, 1954)

Isaac Stern, vln, Symphony of the Air — Leonard Bernstein, Columbia ML 5144; Odyssey Y 34633 — rec. April 19, 1956

Zino Francescatti, vln, New York Philharmonic — Leonard Bernstein, Columbia MS 7058; C.B.S. 72643; 75DC 390-92 (CD — Japan) — rec. July 22, 1965

Serge Blanc, vln, ORTF Philharmonic Orch — Georges Tzipine, SB 001 — pre-1978

Gidon Kremer, vln, Israel Philharmonic Orch — Leonard Bernstein, D.G. 2531196 — rec. 1978

On the Waterfront — film score (1954)

Columbia Pictures Orch — Morris Stoloff, Decca DL 8396; Brunswick LAT 8170 — issued 1956 (5 min. excerpt)

——— love theme

orch — Elmer Bernstein, Dot DLP 3107; DLP 25107; DLP 3364; DLP 25364; Contour 2870182; 2870337 — 1958

(*Continued*)

—————— **symphonic suite** (1960)

New York Philharmonic — Leonard Bernstein, Columbia ML 5651; MS 6251; Philips BBL 7517; SBBL 652; C.B.S. 61096; 62241; 72225; MK 42263 (CD) — rec. May 16, 1960 (love theme issued in M 30304; MLK 39448, CD)

Israel Philharmonic Orch — Leonard Bernstein, D.G. 2532051; 415253 (CD) — rec. May 21-29, 1981

The Lark — choruses for the Anouilh play adapted by Lillian Hellman (1955; f.p. October 28, 1955)

D. Keeling, Tiffin School choir — Walker, Waverley LLP 1039 — rec. 1965 (N.B. 5 Latin choruses only)

Brown-Pembroke chorus — Fidlar, Brown 1000 — 1971 (N.B. 3 French choruses only)

Gregg Smith Singers — Gregg Smith, Vox set SVBX 5353 — rec. 1976

Candide — comic operetta (1956; f.p. in New York Dec. 1, 1956)

CAST	SET A	SET B	SET C
Dr. Pangloss	Max Adrian	Lewis J. Stadler	John Lankston
Candide	Robert Rounseville	Mark Baker	David Eisler
Cunegonde	Barbara Cook	Maureen Brennan	Erie Mills
Old Lady	Irra Petina	June Gable	Joyce Castle

—————— **first version**

(set A) chorus and orch. of the original production — Samuel Krachmalnick, Columbia OL 5180; OS 2350; Philips BBL 7305; B 07399 L; C.B.S. 60337 — rec. Dec. 9, 1956

—————— **second version**

(set B) chorus and orch. of the Chelsea Theater revival — John Mauceri, Columbia set S2X/Q2X 32923 (quad) — rec. March 18–19, 1974 : these two recordings are compared in detail in *Stereo Review*, August 1974, and *High Fidelity*, Sept. 1974.

—————— **third version**

(set C) New York City Opera Chorus and Orch — John Mauceri, New World NW 340/41 (CD) — rec. May 1985

—————— **overture**

Cleveland Pops Orch — Louis Lane, Epic LC 3539; BC 1013; Columbia SX 1583; SCX 3503 — rec. August 21-22, 1958

(Continued)

New York Philharmonic — Leonard Bernstein, Columbia ML 6077; MS 6677; ML 6388; MS 6988; set M2X 895; set D3S 818; M 30304; set M3X 31068; set MG 32174; C.B.S. 72406; set 77244; 71052; 61199-200; 30043; 61816; MK 42263 (CD); MLK 39448 (CD) — rec. Sept. 28, 1960, May 6 & June 18, 1963

Boston Pops Orch — Arthur Fiedler, RCA Victor LM/LSC 2789; ARL 1- 0108; AGL 1-5245; RB/SB 6629 — rec. June 12, 1964

Royal Philharmonic Orch — Eric Rogers, London SPC 21048; Decca PFS 4211; 6.48172; 414382 — 1971

Utah Symphony Orch — Maurice Abravanel, Turnabout TV-S 34459 — 1971

London Symphony Orch — André Previn, Angel S-37021; H.M.V. ASD 2784; ESDW 720 — 1971

Boston Pops Orch — Arthur Fiedler, Polydor 2584002; 2532083 — rec. 1974

Los Angeles Philharmonic Orch — Zubin Mehta, London set CSA 2246; SXL 6811 — rec. May 1975

Boston Pops Orch — John Williams, Philips 416360 (CD) — rec. June 1981

Los Angeles Philharmonic Orch — Leonard Bernstein, D.G. 2532083; 2532085; 413324 (CD); 423169 — rec. 1982

Milwaukee Symphony Orch — Lukas Foss, Pro Arte PAD/CDD 102 (CD) — rec. May 26 – 29, 1983

Philharmonia Virtuosi — Richard Kapp, C.B.S. MK 42125 (CD) — 1986

St. Louis Symphony Orch — Leonard Slatkin, Angel DS-37358; CDC 47522 (CD); EL 270510 — 1986

West Side Story — musical (1957; f.p. in New York Sept. 26, 1957)

CAST	SET A	SET B	SET C	SET D
Maria	Carol Lawrence	Marni Nixon	Lucille Graham	Kiri te Kanawa
Tony	Larry Kert	Jim Bryant	Bruce Trent	José Carreras
Anita	Chita Rivera	Betty Wand	Mary Thomas	Tatiana Troyanos
		Rita Moreno		
Riff	Mickey Calin	Tucker Smith	Joyce Berry	Kurt Ollmann
		Russ Tamblin		
Bernardo	Ken LeRoy	George Chakiris	George Chakiris	

(set A) chorus and orch. of the original production — Max Gober man, Columbia OL 5230; OS 2001; S 32603; CK 32603 (CD); Philips BBL 7277; SBBL 504; B 07362 L; C.B.S. BPG 62060; SBRG 70026; 70025; Embassy 31027 — rec. Sept. 29, 1957

(*Continued*)

(set B) chorus and orch. of the film production — Johnny Green, Columbia OL 5670; OS 2070; Philips BBL 7530; SBBL 659; R 47126 L; 847126 RY; C.B.S. BPG 62058; BRG/SBRG 70006 — rec. 1961 : [N.B. these two recordings are compared in detail in the *American Record Guide*, May 1962.]

(set C) chorus and orch. of the London production — Lawrence Leonard, Saga XIL 6001; ERO 8106 — 1966

(set D) chorus and orch — Leonard Bernstein, D.G. 415253 (CD); Hungaroton SLPDL 12757/58 — rec. Sept. 4 – 7, 1984 (excerpts in 415963, CD)

(excerpts) Deborah Sasson, Peter Hoffman, orch — Michael Tilson Thomas, CBS. FM 39535 — 1985

——— **ballet music**

orch — Robert Prince, Warner B/BS 1240; WM 4003; WS 8003 — 1958

RCA Victor Symphony Orch — Robert Russell Bennett, RCA Victor LM/LSC 2340; RCA Victrola VICS 1491; Camden CDS 1044; KV/KVS 112; VL 84505 — rec. April 8, 1959

——— **symphonic dances**

New York Philharmonic — Leonard Bernstein, Columbia ML 5651; MS 6251; set MG 32174; MK 42263 (CD); Philips BBL 7517; SBB 652; C.B.S. 61096; 62241; 72225; 75DC 390-92 (CD — Japan) — rec. March 6, 1961

Royal Philharmonic Orch — Eric Rogers, London SPC 21048; Decca PFS 4211; 414382 — 1971

San Francisco Symphony Orch — Seiji Ozawa, D.G. 2530309; 2535210; 2531355; 419625 (CD); MHS 512110 (CD) — rec. June 24, 1972

Philadelphia Orch — Eugene Ormandy, RCA Victor ARL 1-0108 — 1973 (Somewhere only)

Atlanta Symphony Orch — Robert Shaw, Vox Cum Laude VCL 9002; MWCD 7122 (CD) — 1981

Los Angeles Philharmonic Orch — Leonard Bernstein, D.G. 2532082; 2532085; 410025 (CD); 423169 — rec. 1982

Kaddish, Symphony No. 3 (1961 – 63/1977; f.p. Dec. 10, 1963)

Felicia Montealegre, speaker, Jennie Tourel, m-s, Camerata Singers (Abraham Kaplan, dir.), Columbus Boychoir (Donald Bryant, dir.), New York Philharmonic — Leonard Bernstein, Columbia KL 6005; KS 6605; set MG 32793; C.B.S. 72265; set 78228 — rec. April 15-17, 1964 (original version)

(*Continued*)

Michael Wager, speaker, Montserrat Caballé, sop, Wiener Jeunesse Chor (Gunter Teuring, dir.), Wiener Sängerknaben (Uwe Harrer, dir.), Israel Philharmonic Orch — Leonard Bernstein, D.G. 2530970; set 2709077; Hungaroton SLPXL 12505 — rec. August 1977

Two Anniversaries (1965)

James Tocco, pf, Pro Arte PAD/CDD 109 (CD); 18038 — rec. March 23 – 27, 1982

Chichester Psalms (1965; f.p. July 15, 1965)

John Bogart, boy alto, Camerata Singers (Abraham Kaplan, dir.), New York Philharmonic — Leonard Bernstein, Columbia ML 6192; MS 6792; C.B.S. 72374 — rec. July 26, l965

[Sängerknabe], alto, Wiener Jeunesse Chor (Günter Teuring, dir.), Israel Philharmonic Orch — Leonard Bernstein, D.G. 2530968; set 2709077; 415965 (CD) — rec. August 1977

Aled Jones, treb, London Symphony Chorus, Royal Philharmonic Orch — Richard Hickox, ASV RPO/CDRPO 8008 (CD); MCA Classics MCAD 6199 — 1986

———— **arranged by the composer for organ and percussion**

James Bowman, ct, King's College Choir of Cambridge — Philip Ledger; with James Lancelot, org, Osian Ellis, hp, David Corkhill, perc, Angel S-37119; H.M.V. ASD 3055 — rec. 1974

Dominic Martelli, treb, Corydon Singers — Matthew Best; with Thomas Trotter, org, Rachel Masters, hp, Gary Kettel, perc, Hyperion A/CDA 66219 (CD) — rec. May 16 – 20, 1986

Shivaree (1970)

brass and percussion ensemble — Frederik Prausnitz, Metropolitan Museum of Art AKS 10001 — 1970

Mass, A Theater Piece for Singers, Players and Dancers (1971; f.p. Sept. 8, 1971)

Alan Titus, David Cryer, Tom Ellis, et al., Norman Scribner Choir, Berkshire Boy Choir, orch. of the original production — Leonard Bernstein, Columbia set M2/M2Q 31008; C.B.S. set 77256 (quad); 50DC 393-94 (CD — Japan) — rec. August – September 1971 (highlights are on MQ 3l960; two meditations are in set MG 32174)

———— **Simple song**

Sherrill Milnes, bar, New Philharmonia Orch — Marcus Dods, RCA Victor ARL 1-0108 — 1973

(*Continued*)

———— Pax — Communion

Philadelphia Orch — Eugene Ormandy, RCA Victor ARL 1-0108 — 1973

———— three meditations

Mstislav Rostropovich, vlc, Israel Philharmonic Orch — Leonard Bernstein, D.G. 2532051; 415966 (CD) — rec. May 21 – 29, 1981

———— excerpts

Boston Pops Orch — Arthur Fiedler, Polydor 2584002 — rec. 1974

Dybbuk — ballet (1974; f.p. May 16, 1974)

David Johnson, bar, John Ostendorf, bass, New York City Ballet Orch — Leonard Bernstein, Columbia M/MQ 33082 (quad); C.B.S. 76486 — rec. June 7, 1974

———— Suites 1 and 2

Paul Sperry, ten, Bruce Fifer, bass, New York Philharmonic — Leonard Bernstein, D.G. 2531348 — rec. 1975

Song Without Words (1974)

James Tocco, pf, Pro Arte PAD/CDD 109 (CD); 18038 — rec. March 23 – 27, 1982

1600 Pennsylvania Avenue — musical (1976; f.p. in New York May 8, 1976)

———— Take care of this house

Frederica von Stade, m-s, National Symphony Orch — Leonard Bernstein, Columbia JC 1 — 1977

Roberta Alexander, sop, Tan Crone, pf, Etcetera ETC/KTC 1037 (CD); MHS 7450 — 1985

Songfest (1977; f.p. October 11, 1977)

Clamma Dale, Rosalind Elias, Nancy Williams, Neil Rosensheim, John Reardon, Donald Gramm, National Symphony Orch — Leonard Bernstein, D.G. 2531044; 415965 (CD) — rec. October 1977

Slava! — overture (1977; f.p. October 11, 1977)

Israel Philharmonic Orch — Leonard Bernstein, D.G. 2532052 — rec. October 1978

Piccolo Serenata (1979)

Roberta Alexander, sop, Tan Crone, pf, Etcetera ETC/KTC 1037 (CD); MHS 7450 — 1985

Touches (1980)

James Tocco, pf, Pro Arte PAD/CDD 109 (CD); 18038 — rec. March 23 – 27, 1982

Bennett Lerner, pf, Etcetera ETC/KTC 1019 (CD); MHS 7513 — 1984

Dag Achatz, pf, BIS CD-352 (CD) — 1986

Divertimento for Orchestra (1980)

Israel Philharmonic Orch — Leonard Bernstein, D.G. 2532052; 415966 (CD) — rec. May 21 – 29, 1981

Bavarian Radio Symphony Orch — Leonard Bernstein, Hungaroton SLPD/HCD 12631 (CD) — rec. 1983

Boston Pops Orch — John Williams, Philips 416360 (CD) — rec. June 1985

A Musical Toast (1980; f.p. in New York October 11, 1980)

Israel Philharmonic Orch — Leonard Bernstein, D.G. 2532052 — rec. May 21 – 29, 1981

Halil, Nocturne for Flute and Small Orchestra (1981; f.p. in Tel Aviv, May 27, 1981)

Jean-Pierre Rampal, fl, Israel Philharmonic Orch — Leonard Bernstein, D.G. 2532051; 415966 (CD) — rec. May 21 – 29, 1981

Moby Dyptich (1981)

James Tocco, pf, Pro Arte PAD/CDD 109 (CD); 18038 — rec. March 23 – 27, 1982

A Quiet Place — opera (1983/1986; f.p. in Houston, June 17, 1983)

Chester Ludgin (Old Sam); Beverly Morgan (Dede); John Brandstetter (Junior); Peter Kazaris (Francois); Jean Kraft (Susie); Theodor Uppman (Bill); Clarity James (Mrs. Doc); John Kuether (Doc); Charles Walker (Funeral Director); Douglas Perry (Analyst); Wendy White (Dinah); Edward Crafts (Young Sam); Louise Edeiken, Mark Thomsen, Kurt Ollman (Trio); ORF Symphony Orch — Leonard Bernstein, D.G. 419761 (CD) — rec. April 1986

Bibliography

I. BOOKS BY LEONARD BERNSTEIN

The Joy of Music (New York: Simon & Schuster, 1959).

Young People's Concerts for Reading and Listening (New York: Simon & Schuster, 1962, revised and enlarged second edition, 1970).

The Infinite Variety of Music (New York: Simon & Schuster, 1966).

The Unanswered Question (Cambridge: Harvard University Press, 1976).

Findings (New York: Simon & Schuster, 1982).

(A bibliography of Bernstein's articles — some of which are reprinted in his books — may be found in Jack Gottlieb's Bernstein catalogue, listed below.)

II. LITERATURE ABOUT LEONARD BERNSTEIN

A. Reference

Jack Gottlieb, ed. *Leonard Bernstein: A Complete Catalogue of His Works* (New York: Boosey & Hawkes, 1978; enlarged second edition, Jalni, 1988).

B. Biographical

Jay Harrison, "Making a Record with Leonard Bernstein," *Reporter* 17 (July 11, 1957), pp. 41–43.

Hope Stoddard, *Symphony Conductors of the U.S.A.* (New York: Crowell, 1957), p. 26–37.

Harold C. Schonberg, "What Bernstein is Doing to the Philharmonic," *Harper's* 218 (May 1959), pp. 43–48.

J. Roddy, "Who lives at Carnegie Hall?" *High Fidelity* 9 (Feb 1959), pp. 32–36+.

David Gow, "Leonard Bernstein, Musician of Many Talents," *Musical Times* 101 (July 1960), pp. 427–429.

David Ewen, *Leonard Bernstein, A Biography for Young People* (Philadelphia: Chilton, 1960).

John Briggs, *Leonard Bernstein, the Man, his Work, and his World* (Cleveland: World, 1961).

Artur Holde, *Leonard Bernstein* (Berlin: Rembrandt, 1961).

Shirley Bernstein, *Making Music: Leonard Bernstein* (Chicago: Encyclopedia Britannica Press, 1963).

John Gruen, with Ken Hyman (photographer), *The Private World of Leonard Bernstein* (New York: Viking, 1968).

Evelyn Ames, *A Wind from the West: Bernstein and the New York Philharmonic Abroad* (Boston: Houghton Mifflin, 1970).

Molly Cone, *Leonard Bernstein* (New York: Thomas Y. Crowell, 1970).

David Wooldridge, *Conductor's World* (New York: Praeger, 1970).

"Leonard Bernstein: An Exclusive Interview," *ASCAP* 6/1 (1972), pp. 6–11.

Robert Chesterman, "Leonard Bernstein in Conversation with Robert Chesterman," *Conversations with Conductors* (London: Robson, 1976), pp. 51–72.

H. K. Jungheinrich, "Der Eklektiker als Pionier," *Musikhandel* 27/6 (1976), p. 264.

G. Shneerson, "Leonard Bernstayn," *Sovetskaya Muzika* 40 (Oct. 1976), pp. 113–121.

John Ardoin, "Leonard Bernstein at Sixty," *High Fidelity/Musical America* 28/8 (1978), p. 53.

Burton Bernstein, *Family Matters* (New York: Summit, 1982).

Helen Matheopoulos, *Maestro: Encounters with Conductors of Today* (New York: Harper & Row, 1982).

David Ewen, *American Composers: A Biographical Dictionary* (New York: G. P. Putnam & Sons, 1982).

Paul Robinson, *Bernstein* (New York: Vanguard, 1982).

Joan Peyser, "Leonard Bernstein," in The New Grove Dictionary of American Music (London: Macmillan, 1986), vol. I, pp. 195–200.

Joan Peyser, *Bernstein* (New York: Morrow, 1987).

C. Critical: General

Peter Gradenwitz, "Leonard Bernstein," *Music Review* X (1949), 191–202.

Jack Gottlieb, *The Music of Leonard Bernstein: A Study of Melodic Manipulations* (doctoral dissertation, University of Illinois, 1964).

W. W. Tromble, *The American Intellectual and Music: An Analysis of the Writings of Suzanne K. Langer, Paul Henry Lang, Jacques Barzun, John Dewey, and Leonard Bernstein — with Implications for Music Education at the College Level* (doctoral dissertation, University of Michigan, 1968).

Jack Gottlieb, "Symbols of Faith in the Music of Leonard Bernstein," *Musical Quarterly* 66 (1980), p. 287.

Abraham, Lubin, "The Influence of Jewish Music and Thought in the Works of Leonard Bernstein" [in Hebrew, summary in English], *Tatzlil* [The Chord] no. 20 (1980), pp. 35–39.

Linda J. Snyder, *Leonard Bernstein's Work for the Musical Theatre: How the Music Functions Dramatically* (D.M.A. dissertation, University of Illinois, 1982).

U. Schneider, "Die Wiedergeburt der Musik aus dem Geist des Dreiklangs — Leonard Bernstein als verbaler Musikdeuter," *HiFi Stereophonie* 21/1 (1982), p. 56.

James W. Moore, *A Study of Tonality in Selected Works by Leonard Bernstein* (Ph.D. dissertation, Florida State University, 1984).

Peter Gradenwitz, *Leonard Bernstein* (Zurich: Atlantis, 1984).

Samuel Lipman, "Lenny on our Minds," *New Criterion* 3/10 (1985), p. 1.

D. Critical: Specific works

Candide

Brooks Atkinson, "Musical 'Candide'," *New York Times* (Dec. 9, 1956), Section 2, p. 5.

Wolcott Gibbs, "Voltaire Today," *The New Yorker* 32 (Dec. 15, 1956), p. 52.

"The Opulent Optimist," *Opera News* 21 (Feb 11, 1957), 24.

Robert Jacobson and Leighton Kerner, "New York", *Opera News* 38 (Feb. 9, 1974), pp. 33–35.

Vaclac Nelhybel, "Time in your hands" (*Candide* overture), *Instrument* 32 (Sept. 1977), pp. 47–49.

Choral music

Jack Gottlieb, "The Choral Music of Leonard Bernstein, Reflections of Theater and Liturgy," *American Choral Review* 10 (1968), pp. 155–177.

The Dybbuk

M. L. Sokol, "The Dybbuk in music," *Hobbies* 80 (March 1975), 35–36.

Bayan Northcott and Oliver Knussen, "Recordings" [Dybbuk], *Tempo* no. 119 (Dec. 1976), p. 34.

Alan Jay Pearlmutter, *Leonard Bernstein's* Dybbuk: *An Analysis Including Historical, Religious, and Literary Perspectives of Hasidic Life and Lore* (D.M.A. dissertation, Peabody Institute of Johns Hopkins University, 1985).

Ḥalil

Andrew Porter, "Musical Events," *The New Yorker* 58 (April 26, 1982), p. 112.

Mass

W. Bender, "A Mass for everyone, maybe," *Time* 98 (Sept. 20, 1971), pp. 41–43.

Shirley Fleming, "At JFK Center," *High Fidelity/Musical America* 21 (Dec. 1971), pp. MA10–11.

Irving Lowens, "Washington," *Musical Times* 112 (Dec. 1971), pp. 1192–1193.

Irving Kolodin, "Recordings in Review: Bernstein's Mass Revisited," *Saturday Review* 54 (Dec. 25, 1971), p. 55.

"Leonard Bernstein discusses his Mass with High Fidelity," *High Fidelity/Musical America* 22 (Feb. 1972), pp. 68–70.

David Hamilton, "Mass and the Press," *High Fidelity/Musical America* 22 (Feb. 1972), pp. 74–76.

Irving Lowens and A. Hays, "Choral performances," *American Choral Review* 14/3 (1972), pp. 37–39.

H. Berlinski, "Bernstein's Mass," *Sacred Music* 99/1 (1972), p. 3.

John Gruen, "In Love With the Stage," *Opera News* 37/5 (1972), p. 16–23.

N. Goemanne, "Open Forum: the Controversial Bernstein Mass.: Another Point of View," *Sacred Music* 100/1 (1973), p. 33.

F. O. Beck, "Open forum: Re: Bernstein's Mass — 'You cannot make a silk purse out of a sow's ear'," *Sacred Music* 100/4 (1973), p. 32.

G. Brunner, "Ein fundamentales Missverständnis: Bernsteins 'Mass' im Konzertsaal und auf der Schallplatte," *Opernwelt* no. 8 (Aug. 1973), pp. 34–36.

Clytus Gottwald, "Leonard Bernsteins Messe oder der Konstruktion der Blasphemie," *Melos/NZM* 2/4 (1976), pp. 281–284.

William A. Cottle, *Social Commentary in Vocal Music in the Twentieth Century as Evidenced by Leonard Bernstein's* Mass (D.A. dissertation, University of Northern Colorado, 1978).

Gary DeSesa, *A Comparison Between Descriptive Analysis of Leonard Bernstein's* Mass *and the Musical Implications of the Critical Evaluations Thereof* (Ph.D. dissertation, New York University, 1985).

On the Waterfront

William Hamilton, "On the Waterfront," *Film Music* xiv/1 (1954), p. 3–14.

Hans Keller, "On the Waterfront," *Score*, no. 12 (1955), p. 81–84.

John Huntley, "Music in films," *Musical Times* 98 (Dec. 1957), pp. 662–663.

Peter Pan

C. Smith, "Peter Pan. Barrie's Peter Pan with Bernstein Songs," *Musical America* 70 (May 1950), p. 4.

Serenade for violin, strings, and percussion

Massimo Mila, "Lettera da Venezia," *La Rassegna Musicale* 24 (Oct.–Dec. 1954), p. 351.

Edward Downes, "Serenade for violin solo, strings and percussion" (recording), *Musical Quarterly* 43 (Apr. 1957), pp. 266–268.

Leonard J. Lehrman, *Leonard Bernstein's Serenade after Plato's Symposium: An Analysis* (D.M.A. thesis, Cornell University, 1977).

Piano Music

Sigrid Luther, *The* Anniversaries *for Solo Piano by Leonard Bernstein* (D.M.A. dissertation, Louisiana State University, 1986).

A Quiet Place

Leighton Kerner, "Truth in Tahiti," *Village Voice* 28 (July 5, 1983), p. 79.

Andrew Porter, "Musical Events," *The New Yorker* 59 (July 11, 1983), pp. 88–89.

Gregory Sandow, "Made-for-TV Opera (at Kennedy Center)," *Village Voice* 29 (August 14, 1984), pp. 75–76.

Leighton Kerner, "The Fearsome Garden," *Village Voice* 29 (August 21, 1984), pp. 102–3.

1600 Pennsylvania Avenue

J. Beaufort, "Bubbly Bernstein: composer teams with Lerner in new musical," *Christian Science Monitor* (May 7, 1976), p. 32.

Brendan Gill, "Juggernaut," *The New Yorker* 52 (May 17, 1976), p. 124.

Irving Kolodin, "Music Returns to the Musical," *Saturday Review* 3 (Apr. 3, 1976), pp. 43–45.

G. H. Wilk, "New York: Musicals, musicals," *Bühne* no. 213 (June 1976), pp. 32–34.

Symphonies

"*Jeremiah* Symphony; *Age of Anxiety*," *Notes* 7 (Sept. 1950), pp. 626–627.

"Symphony No. 2 (The Age of Anxiety)", *Music Review* 13 (May 1952), pp. 157–158.

Peter G. Davis, "Bernstein as Symphonist," *New York Times* (Nov. 26, 1978), Section II, p. 17.

C. L. Osborne, "Bernstein's Third Symphony," *Musical Times* 105 (Aug. 1964), p. 599.

Jack Gottlieb, "Leonard Bernstein: 'Kaddish Symphony'," *Perspectives of New Music* 4/1 (1965), pp. 171–175.

David E. Boelzner, *The Symphonies of Leonard Bernstein: An Analysis of Motivic Character* (M.A. thesis, University of North Carolina, 1977).

Trouble in Tahiti

G. B. Jackson, "Trouble in Tahiti," *Opera News* 17 (Oct. 27, 1952), 13.

Leonard Burkat, "Current Chronicle: Boston (Trouble in Tahiti)," *Musical Quarterly* 39 (1953), pp. 94–98.

The Unanswered Question (Norton lectures)

Alan Keiler, "Bernstein's *The Unanswered Question* and Problems of Musical Competence," *Musical Quarterly* 64 (1978), p. 195

David Hamilton, "The Unanswered Question: why?", *High Fidelity/Musical America* 25 (Apr. 1975), pp. 71–73.

West Side Story

Brooks Atkinson, "West Side Story," *New York Times* (Oct. 6, 1957), Section 2, p. 1.

Howard Taubman, "A foot in each camp," *New York Times* (Oct. 13, 1957), Section 2, p. 9.

"'West Side Story' as an Experiment in Method," *New York Times* (Oct. 27, 1957), Section 2, p. 15.

"Dancing Dominates new Broadway Show," *Musical America* 77 (Nov. 1, 1957), 11–12.

Mary Rhoads, *Leonard Bernstein's West Side Story* (M.F.A. thesis, University of Michigan, 1964).

Gertrude Jackson, "*West Side Story*: Thema, Grundhaltung und Aussage," *Maske und Kothurn* 16 (1970), pp. 97–101.

J. Novick, "In search of a new consensus (how Broadway musicals reflect the times)," *Saturday Review* 3 (Apr. 3, 1976), pp. 39–42.

Wonderful Town

Brooks Atkinson, "Wonder town," *New York Times* (March 8, 1953), Section II, p. 1.

Howard Taubman, "Tunesmith of 'Wonderful Town'," *New York Times* (Apr. 5, 1953), Section II, p. 1.

Olin Downes, "Wonderful time," *New York Times* (May 10, 1953), Section II, p. 7

David Drew, "Leonard Bernstein: *Wonderful Town*," *Score* no. 12 (1955), pp. 77–80.

Patrick J. Smith, "New York," *Opera* [England] 34 (January 1983), pp. 47–48.

Robert Jacobsen, "New York," *Opera News* 47 (January 1, 1983), pp. 37–38.

Photo Credits